The World According to
HARRY

Also by Harry Redknapp

Always Managing
A Man Walks On To a Pitch
It Shouldn't Happen To a Manager

The World According to
HARRY

HARRY REDKNAPP
WITH BEN DIRS

EBURY
PRESS

1 3 5 7 9 10 8 6 4 2

Ebury Press, an imprint of Ebury Publishing
20 Vauxhall Bridge Road
London SW1V 2SA

Ebury Press is part of the Penguin Random House group of companies
whose addresses can be found at global.penguinrandomhouse.com

 Penguin
Random House
UK

First published by Ebury Press in 2019

www.penguin.co.uk

A CIP catalogue record for this book is available from the British Library

ISBN 9781529104905
TPB ISBN: 9781529104912

Typeset in 11/18 pt ITC Galliard Std
by Integra Software Services Pvt. Ltd, Pondicherry

Printed and bound in Great Britain by Clays Ltd, Elcograf S.p.A.

 Penguin Random House is committed to a sustainable future
for our business, our readers and our planet. This book is
made from Forest Stewardship Council® certified paper.

To my grandchildren, who persuaded me to do
I'm a Celebrity ... Get Me Out of Here!

CONTENTS

1

JUNGLE DRUMS

'What's the worst that can happen?'

On my first day in the jungle for *I'm a Celebrity ... Get Me Out of Here*, I found myself looking around the camp and thinking, 'I'm a football manager. How on earth did I end up here?' I honestly thought it would be hard work, sitting around all day with people I didn't know and didn't seem to have anything in common with. 'My God,' I thought, 'what have I got myself into? I'm not sure I'm going to last too long ... '

I spent most of that first day listening to the others chatting away and because they were mainly showbiz people, actors, singers or presenters, I didn't have a clue what they were going on about. Rita Simons, Sair Khan and Malique Thompson-Dwyer were in soap operas,

Emily Atack was in a sitcom, Fleur East was a singer, James McVey was in a band, Nick Knowles was a TV presenter, John Barrowman was an entertainer and Anne Hegerty was off a quiz show. So most of the conversation revolved around television programmes, pop music or who was appearing in this or that in the West End. It was all going over my head, and I did wonder if I'd have anything to offer.

At one point, they started talking about what they listened to on the radio, and when I said talkSPORT, they were all scratching their heads. John said to me, 'What's talkSPORT?'

'You know, talkSPORT, with Alan Brazil and the other lads.'

'Yeah, but what is it?'

'Well, they talk about sport ...'

It was only Nick who had heard of it, and even he didn't have much interest in sport. When I started talking about Harry Kane, Nick and James were the only two who knew who he was. I couldn't get my head around that: Harry Kane had just won the Golden Boot at the World Cup!

When I'm not in the jungle, I chat to my mates about football or horse racing or golf, but this wasn't my normal crowd. They were completely different people to the kind I was used to mixing with and it was like suddenly living on another planet. And to think I could have been waltzing around a ballroom back in London ...

That's right, I was also asked to do *Strictly Come Dancing*. God knows why. At a meeting with the programme makers, I came straight out with it.

'I can't do *Strictly*. For a start, I can't dance.'

'Don't worry about that, Harry, we'll send a dancer over so you can practise.'

So they sent Amy Dowden over, this lovely girl from Wales. They booked a hall for us at Meyrick Park golf club, but I said, 'I can't go up there, all the blokes know me. Imagine me dancing around and they're all looking through the window and laughing.' So we ended up dancing in the house – the cha-cha-cha and the quickstep – with my wife Sandra laughing at me instead. Actually, she said I was better than she expected. But that's not really saying much.

I'm not really one for getting up and dancing at weddings. I might do a quick waltz with Sandra at the end, but that's about my limit. So after giving it some thought, I decided to give *Strictly* a miss. I'd have been out of my depth and ended up as the clown, like they have in every series. I didn't really want to be that person who was tripping over, being slaughtered by the judges but not getting voted off every week because the public felt sorry for me.

However, somebody from *I'm a Celebrity* got wind that I'd turned *Strictly* down and asked if I'd do the jungle instead. They'd already asked a few times but this time my grandkids found out about it and started driving me mad. They kept pulling my arm and saying, 'Please, Pop, you'll love it! And don't be scared of Kiosk Kev!'

'Who's Kiosk Kev?'

'He's the man who owns the Outback Shack. You go to him when you win a Dingo Dollar Challenge. He's really mean.'

'Oh, right . . . '

I hadn't even seen the programme, not one minute of it. But Sandra had watched it over the years and when I was wavering as to whether to do it or not, she started telling me how upset the grandkids would be if I decided not to. Then I had a round of golf with a couple of mates whose opinions I value, and they said I'd be mad not to do it. In the end I thought, 'You know what, I'll give it a go. I might be 71, but it will be a new experience at my age, something different. The worst that can happen is that I meet some different people.'

It's not like I had any real commitments. Don't get me wrong, I like to keep myself busy, whether it's following the horses, playing golf or keeping tabs on new property I'm involved in. But my biggest decision most days is whether to have a sausage or bacon sandwich in the café down the road. People used to tell me I'd drive Sandra mad when I stopped managing, but I've never been more relaxed and I've loved every minute of it. When I open my eyes in the morning I think, 'Thank God there'll be no aggravation today.'

Once I'd put pen to paper, Sandra kept saying, 'You've got to watch some old episodes of the programme, so that you know what you've let yourself in for.'

That didn't sound promising. So I said to her, 'No, if I watch it, I probably won't do it.'

'You don't get any food. Are you sure you're going to be alright?'

One minute Sandra was telling me to go in, the next she was telling me how terrible it was going to be.

'Sandra,' I said, 'there's no way they're going to put celebrities in a jungle with no food. They can't starve us. I've done adverts and stuff, it will be like that. What happens is, they'll have a caravan round the back where you can have a cup of coffee and a bacon sandwich. We'll all be sitting about making out we're hungry, someone will take us back to the caravan, and once we've polished off breakfast, they'll send us back in. We'll go back to sitting on the logs, pretending we're hungry, and the viewers won't even notice we've been gone.'

'No, Harry, I don't think they will … '

Unfortunately, Sandra went down with sepsis just before I was due to fly over to Australia. I was driving back from London when my daughter-in-law phoned to tell me Sandra had been taken to hospital. Sepsis is a dangerous illness, and if they had kept her waiting in A&E, it could have been very serious. It can take a grip very fast and be lethal if it's not treated immediately.

She was in and out for treatment and tests after that, and if she hadn't been 100 per cent right, I wouldn't have gone in the jungle. I was umming and ahing until a few days before my flight, when Sandra decided she felt well enough for me to go. I said to the producers, 'If you get word that Sandra isn't good, I've got to know straightaway, because I'll have to come out.' But I did end up flying out to Australia, and the rest is history.

When I got off the plane, I went through customs and there was this massive guy to meet me. He was like an All Black rugby player, one of the biggest people I'd ever seen. He shook my hand and said to me, 'You're now in lockdown. Can I have your phone?'

'But I have to make a call. I have to tell my wife that I won't be able to ring her, because you've taken my phone off me.'

'Okay. Just the one … '

So I phoned Sandra and told her I wouldn't be able to speak to her until I got out of the jungle. And this was a week before I actually went into the jungle. My son Jamie didn't even know I was going in until a few days before it started. It was all very cloak and dagger, as if I'd parachuted in behind enemy lines.

At the hotel, which was miles from anywhere, I had a chaperone looking after me. There was no one else from the programme staying there – we were all in separate places, so that none of us would have a clue who was going in. Tina was a lovely lady from New Zealand who'd been chaperoning contestants for eight or nine series, and she was in the room next door. So on the first morning, I got up at about six o'clock and thought I'd have a nice cup of coffee and some breakfast, grab a sunbed and lie by the pool. But as soon as I opened my door, Tina popped out of her room and said, 'Where do you think you're going, Harry?'

I couldn't believe it. It was like being held hostage. A couple of mornings I managed to sneak out and grab half an hour to myself, but Tina would always catch me and drag me back inside.

One day, Tina took me to this shopping centre because I needed to buy some swimming shorts to take into the jungle. While we were wandering around, I said to her, 'There's an Italian restaurant over there. I like Italian, why don't we have dinner there?' She took a bit of persuading, because I wasn't meant to have dinner anywhere but inside the hotel, but she eventually agreed. So that night, we walked into this Italian and it was lovely, absolutely buzzing. And no sooner were we through the door than the head waiter comes marching towards us with his arms wide open and a big grin on his face. It turned out that he was Croatian and absolutely mad about football.

'Ah, Mr Redknapp! You managed all my favourite players: Luka Modrić, Robert Prosinečki, Davor Šuker! Great to see you! What would you like to drink?'

'I'd like a nice glass of red wine.'

'And your wife?'

'No, she's not my wife.'

The waiter gave me a sly smile and a wink.

'Oh, it's like that is it, Harry … '

'No, really, it's nothing like that.'

'Okay, Harry, no problem, your secret is safe with me … '

The food was lovely, so I dragged Tina there every night. And every time we walked in, this Croatian guy was winking at me and chuckling under his breath, as if to say, 'You naughty boy, Harry … ' He obviously thought I was having a dirty week away with my mistress, and I couldn't tell him why I was really there.

By the time the week was up, I couldn't wait to escape the hotel and get into the jungle. That's not a sentence I thought I'd ever say. I was miles out of my comfort zone already. But you know what? I was kind of enjoying it.

2
GROWING UP HAPPY

'Nothing in life is inevitable ... '

My dad was a docker who worked on the West India Docks all his life. He had my name down to go and work on the docks from when I was about eight years old. In those days, you had to pay something like a penny or tuppence a week to keep a place open, because that's just what the son of a docker was expected to do. As well as my dad and his twin brother Georgie, my grandfather was a docker and all my mum's family were dockers. Georgie was a crane driver – or, more correctly, a dangerous crane driver, because he liked to have a drink while he was on the job. So my only realistic ambition was to go and work with my dad and uncle on the Isle of Dogs. And that wasn't just my ambition, that was the ambition of everyone at my school. But just because your life is already mapped out for you, that doesn't mean you have to follow the signs.

My mum worked in a local cake factory and cleaned offices in Aldgate. Her mum, who was called Maggie Brown, used to collect all the bets off the old girls on her street, back when that was illegal. I think it's safe to say that it was my nan who got me hooked on the horses. It wasn't exactly big time, the normal bet would be a tuppenny double or tuppenny treble, and my nan would wrap up all the individual bets and stick them on the mantelpiece until the bookmaker came round to collect them. We called the bookie Cyril the Paper Boy, even though he must have been about 70. He always wore a suit and tie and a trilby hat, like a proper little East End chap. Cyril would come round shouting, '*Star* and *Standard*!' and my nan would take a newspaper off him and drop the money into his satchel.

Sometimes, I'd get home from school to find my nan being dragged off to the police station again. She'd say to me, 'Don't worry, boy, your dinner's in the oven. I'll be back in an hour,' and then disappear off in the back of a Black Maria. They'd give her a slap on the wrist, tell her to knock it on the head, and she'd be back doing exactly the same thing the next day.

Maggie was a lovely old girl and a fantastic character. She'd hand me the newspaper and say, ''Ere y'are, boy, pick out the three you want.' I'd put a circle around three horses, she'd rub the paper on the top of my head – 'Ginger for luck!' – and then she'd put on a tuppenny treble bet. We didn't have a television, but we got the racing results at six o'clock in the evening. The next day, Cyril would come back, pay out whoever had won and take another round of bets.

From living in a couple of rooms above my great-grandmother's house on Barchester Street, we moved to the Burdett Estate in Poplar. Barchester Street had bomb sites at both ends, which were once houses, and some of the houses that hadn't been hit were falling down anyway. So our new flat was like paradise. Our old flat had an outside toilet in the yard. It didn't have a fridge, so we'd have to put food and milk outside, which wasn't great in the summer. We didn't have central heating or electricity. Instead, we had gas mantles on the walls. We didn't even have a bathroom, we had a tin bath that hung on the wall outside the back door. We'd stick it in front of the fire and pour a couple of saucepans of hot water in. The water would only be about four inches high. If anyone was having a bath, everyone else would have to go in the other room.

My first school was Susan Lawrence Primary, which had a couple of enthusiastic sports teachers called Mr Enniver and Mr Clark, who both loved their football. But other than sport, there was nothing for me at school. If you were clever enough to pass the 11-plus, you went to the local grammar school. If you were just average, you went to something called a central school. But if you were an idiot like me, you went to a secondary modern, where the education was secondary and nothing was modern.

Sir Humphrey Gilbert really was the worst secondary school in the East End. I swear some people think I'm exaggerating when I say how bad that school was, but it was absolutely horrendous. In fact, it was more like a nuthouse than a school, a rough and dangerous place. Student teachers would get dumped there, run out crying or screaming after one day and we'd never see them again. Pupils at Humphrey Gilbert didn't go to school in the way that other kids went to school. We did no work and learnt nothing. Instead, we turned up late, caused mayhem, got the cane and went home again.

We had to be in school at nine o'clock for assembly, but after about a week, I realised that they didn't even take our names. So instead of going to assembly, I'd spend an hour in the toilets with all the truants and go straight to my first lesson at ten. The other kids were mostly 14 or 15 and I was only 11.

There were only a couple of teachers we were scared of and who could keep some semblance of control. Mr Merton used to give us the cane. He'd tell you to put your hand out and the natural thing to do was pull your hand away just as he was about to hit you. But he wouldn't let you go until he'd give you six of the best. It was never for anything serious, mainly just messing around in class. I used to act up in Wood and Metalwork, really wind up the teacher, Mr Harris. He'd drag me out to the front of the class, bend me over and whack me on the bum. What he didn't know was that I'd put wire wool down the back of my trousers, so while I was pretending to be hurt, I wouldn't feel a thing.

Another time, we were playing a football match against our big rivals Hay Currie over at Hackney Marshes, and Mr Harris was the referee. I was only 11 or 12 but playing for the under-15s. We had matching shirts but, believe it or not, no shorts or socks. So we played in army boots and jeans. We won the game, but Mr Harris gave a couple of dodgy decisions. After the final whistle, a couple of lads, who went on to be proper villains, started booting

Mr Harris's moped as he was trying to drive off. They pushed him off and smashed his wheels. I didn't get involved, because they were big lads and their reputations preceded them. And poor Mr Harris was scared out of his wits.

The kids at Humphrey Gilbert didn't bother and most of the teachers didn't care because everyone knew they were heading for the docks anyway. If not the docks, working in a factory. That was just the way it was going to be. If they gave you a piece of paper to write on, you'd make an aeroplane out of it.

The upshot was that lots of kids left school without being able to read or write. I wasn't much better. When I did my coaching badges, I had to do a written test about the laws of the game. I failed it and had to re-sit a few months later. I might have failed again if the bloke in charge hadn't decided to give me all the answers. I was useless at school, failed everything to do with books, not that we had many. I left school at the age of 14 completely uneducated, without a clue about anything. Even today, I can barely string a sentence together. And beyond being able to sign an autograph and write 'best wishes', my handwriting is awful, not much different to a six-year-old's.

But just because I didn't get an education didn't mean I wasn't happy. The East End was a different world back then. You had to be streetwise and it was a case of just trying to survive, but it was also a great place to grow up. The Burdett Estate was something like 20 blocks of flats with a school in the middle. Behind the flats was a bit of grass we nicknamed Wembley and we'd be on there every night playing football until it got too dark to see. It was our own little enclosed world, a safe place to be. A plastic ball cost about six shillings and whoever had one was king. You'd hear the shout go out, 'Big game at Wembley!' and within minutes there would be hundreds of kids out on that bit of grass, pretending they were the football stars of the day. Only when you heard your mum shouting your name did you go in for dinner.

Almost everything I learnt as a footballer came from my time playing on that little patch of grass. Even when it got dark early in the winter, we'd play head tennis in the bike shed, which had a light inside. Because there would be so many kids on each team, you had to be good at dribbling, otherwise you might not see the ball again. Because of that, there were loads of dribblers back then. Now, all coaches talk about is passing, passing, passing.

The caretakers – or porters, as we called them – would try to throw us off the grass all the time. One night, this tough old docker called Albert Chamberlain was leaning over the balcony watching us play when one of the porters started shouting at us to stop and threatening to grass us up to our mums. Albert shouted down, 'Why don't you fuckin' leave 'em alone? What 'arm are they doin'?' The porter left us alone after that, probably because he was scared of Albert. But soon afterwards, Albert decided to start up a team.

He called us Burdett Boys, got hold of some kit and he entered us into the Regent's Boys League. Regent's Park is over in north-west London, which seemed like the other end of the world to a load of ten-year-old kids. We'd have to leave the estate at 6.30 in the morning, get a bus, jump on a tube and change a couple of times. When we got there, we'd have to walk across the park and get changed on the side of the pitch, because there were no changing rooms. It was an under-11s league, so we used to get hammered every week.

But Albert strengthened the team, and we started turning the tide. We switched leagues and started playing on Hackney Marshes, which was a lot more convenient and also meant that good kids from the East End started joining from other teams. Lots of kids who played for Burdett Boys ended up signing pro contracts. Terry Reardon and Roger Hoy went to Tottenham, Georgie Jacks and John Blake went to QPR, and me and Colin Mackleworth ended up at West Ham.

There were no computer games in those days and hardly anyone had a television, so no wonder everyone played football. I'd play for East London on the Saturday, Burdett Boys under-11s on the Sunday morning and then play for the older team in the afternoon. I also played for East London Schools at cricket. One game, when I was about 14, I took nine wickets for six runs and won a prize for schoolboy bowling performance of the week in the *Star* newspaper. I've still got the prize ball. When my mum died and I cleared out her house, I found it in a drawer, all shiny and new. I also came third in the 400m in the London Schools Championships. I didn't really like running, but I was good at it and the teachers pushed me into it. All the other kids had spikes, but I ran in my slippers. The track was cinder, so I was slipping and sliding all over the place. I only got beat by a yard, so could have won easily.

But football was always my first love. Every Christmas, I'd get something to do with football, often a new pair of Stanley Matthews or Tom Finney boots. There were no replica kits in those days, they came along much later. I was an only child and used to follow my dad all over London watching him play. He was a very good amateur player, good enough to be a professional. But he went into the army at 16, got taken prisoner during the war and by the time he got out, his chance had gone. He was a wizard with the ball, miles better than any of the lads he played with. Even in his 50s he would run rings around us kids.

Dad also loved watching football. Wherever there was a game on, he'd be there. He'd stand out on the balcony in front of the flat, and if the lights came on at East London Stadium at half-past six, he'd be over there like a shot. My mum would say, 'Thank God for that, I can watch *Coronation Street* in peace ... ' But watching all that football meant he had an incredible eye for talent. When I was managing West Ham, I was driving home from the ground when my mobile rang. It was my dad, who'd just been watching the youth team.

He said to me, 'I've just watched the best kid I've ever seen play.'

'Who?'

'Kid in midfield. Never seen anything like it.'

'Young Frank Lampard?'

'No. Frank was good, but this other kid was different class.'

'What was his name?'

'Boy called Ferdinand ... '

I didn't even know Rio Ferdinand was playing. But after my dad's phone call, I kept a close eye on him. And when he turned 16, we signed him, before turning him into one of the best defenders this country has ever produced.

In those days, people would follow individual players, and my dad was a big Tom Finney fan. Finney played for Preston, but if he was playing at Chelsea, we'd go to Stamford Bridge. If he was playing at Arsenal, we'd go to Highbury. Or we might go and see Stanley Matthews playing at West Ham.

My dad supported Arsenal and he'd take me to Highbury a lot. My Uncle Jim was also a massive Arsenal fan and, as a kid, my biggest heroes were Arsenal players, people like Jimmy Bloomfield and Danny Clapton. Football was less tribal in those days, so I also loved Vic Keeble and Johnny Dick, who were West Ham's strike partnership. They went together like bacon and eggs.

When I started at West Ham, Dick was just coming to the end of his career. He was a lovely man, a fantastic character and a maniac gambler who'd bet on anything. I remember seeing Arsenal lose 6–0 to West Ham at Upton Park in 1960, when Dave Dunmore scored a hat-trick. And we also went to watch Tottenham, Charlton and Millwall, which was traditionally the dockers' club. We'd wait at the entrance of the Rotherhithe Tunnel and thumb a lift across the river. I also saw the last game Manchester United's 'Busby Babes' played in England before the Munich air disaster, when they beat Arsenal 5–4 at Highbury in 1958. Bobby Charlton scored that day, as did Tommy Taylor and the great Duncan Edwards. Five days later, Tommy was dead and Duncan died from his injuries two weeks later.

He could be a bit of a rogue, my dad. He'd always go out on the booze on Christmas Eve, with his mates from work. One year, he was supposed to pick up a chicken from the butcher's on Christmas Eve (we didn't have turkeys in those days) but ended up knocking off work and going straight to the pub instead. Either that or he picked it up and lost it. Me and Mum ended up traipsing all over Poplar looking for him. Eventually, we found him in the Earl of Ellesmere, having a knees-up with the girls from the nearby cake factory. Mum kicked him all the way home. On Christmas morning, we had to go down Petticoat Lane and buy a chicken from a Jewish butcher. He got that wrong as well – he bought a boiling chicken instead of a roasting chicken, and it was like eating string. If I remember rightly, my mum hit him round the head with it.

But they were good people, my mum and dad. I grew up poor, but I grew up happy. And because of Dad's passion for football, what seemed unavoidable – that I would spend my working life on the docks – turned into a more exciting life. Which just goes to show, nothing in life has to be inevitable.

3
KEEPING IT REAL

'I'm not looking for mates who are millionaires ...'

Since I've been out of the jungle, it's been non-stop. The response has been amazing. Before going on the show, all anyone ever wanted to talk to me about was football, football, football. Now all anyone wants to talk about is the jungle: 'Congratulations! How was it in there, Harry? What's Noel Edmonds really like? We didn't miss an episode. I voted for you to win it! Yabba Dabba Doo!' But it doesn't get on my nerves. Far from it. I'm just a normal fella, and proud of it.

I went shopping in Marks & Spencer and ladies were coming up to me and shouting, 'Harry, emu's in the other aisle!' Or they'd say,

'What are you shopping for, jam roly-polies?' because I'd mentioned how much I loved them on the show. People were sending me jam roly-polies in the post, addressed simply to 'Harry Redknapp, Poole'. Me and Sandra were thinking about opening a jam roly-poly stall on the market and I was waiting for someone who makes jam roly-polies to ask me to appear in one of their adverts. Sandra warmed them up, made a load of custard and we handed them out to the homeless in Bournemouth. As well as the jam roly-polies we got sent, me and Sandra went out and bought a load so that nobody went without.

If people are nice to me, I'm nice to them. If anyone is cocky or bolshie or bombastic, I might get the hump with them. I've got no time for snobbery or people who think they're better than anyone else. In fact, I absolutely hate people who talk to waiters like shit or talk down to workmen or cleaners or anybody who does a job that doesn't make them rich or 'important'.

On the way back from Australia, we stopped off in Dubai. There were all these lovely Indian waiters and this Russian bloke was talking to them like dirt. I hated seeing it. Another time, Clement Freud, the former politician and writer, interviewed me over dinner at Plumpton Racecourse. When someone came over and asked for my autograph, Freud said, 'Why don't you piss off and not be so rude?' I was so embarrassed, just wanted the ground to swallow me up. I said to the bloke, 'No, don't worry, I'll sign it.' A little while later, a waitress came over and he said the same thing to her. I found it disgusting that he'd talk to people like that. It's just not in my nature. I don't care if I'm eating my dinner or not. I don't sit there thinking, 'My food's getting cold.' I'll still sign an autograph and have a bit of a chat. It's not a problem to me.

I'm comfortable with people talking to me – I talk to everyone. My old man was the same, he gave everyone the time of day. And I'm happier talking to the man or woman on the street than anybody else. I'll say good morning to people when I pass them on the street. I'll have a chat with the guy in the shop when I buy my newspaper. In the morning, I'll pop in the café over the road from the house, have some bacon and eggs, read my *Racing Post* and have a chat with whoever happens to be in there: 'You down on holiday for a few days? How's your mum? What's your boy up to?' A lot of the time, I don't even know who they are. I'll be driving along, hit traffic and there will be a little kid in the car next to me, wanting to take my picture. So I'll open my window and give him a thumbs-up. When I go up to the car wash, I'll take a bag of donuts and say, ''Ere y'are lads, have one of these with your tea.' They work hard and they deserve it, and it only costs me a couple of quid. And my favourite people are London cabbies, I absolutely love them. When I jump in a London cab, I won't just sit there and say nothing for 20 minutes, I'll chat to them about football or racing or anything they fancy, as if I'm one of their mates.

It's very important to me that I've never changed or forgotten my roots. I'm not looking for mates who are millionaires, so I've still got lots of friends from the East End, including people I went to school with. I might live in a nice house on the south coast, but East Enders are still my people. I've got mates who work on Billingsgate Fish Market. My best mate, Tony Lewis, drives a black cab. We've been mates since we were eight or nine, living on the Burdett Estate. When my last book came out, a boy came to one of the signings and asked me to sign a copy for his dad. When he told me his dad's name, I remembered we grew up together. So I got his number and popped round his house for a cup of tea and some biscuits. And that cup of tea and those biscuits were better than a slap-up meal in London's poshest restaurant.

Sandra's always said that I make people feel like I know them, even when I don't. I'm a bit of an old softy really. If there's something I can do to help someone, I'll do it. People will phone me up and say, 'Harry, there's something on at Poole hospital, any chance you can come down?' I'm a real sucker for that kind of stuff. Over the years, I've had women dressed as schoolgirls taking penalties against me, served up chips in schools and opened just about anything you can imagine, from garden fetes to charity shops. If I can make someone happy, why not? But I've always had journalists who write up interviews with me and make me sound like a cross between Del Boy and Ronnie Kray. That's what the media like to do, turn you into a caricature.

When I was managing, I'd often make training sessions open house. I'd let kids in who were sick or had terminal illnesses. When I was at West Ham, I'd let all the old boys come and watch us train. There would be 50 or 60 on the touchline some days, people who had been watching the club all their lives. I like to do what I can for various charities, whether it's helping to organise golf days or finding prizes for auctions. When I was manager at Tottenham, I'd put up a day watching us train and meeting the players. The players would enjoy it and the kids would be over the moon at talking to their heroes. I'd also do appearances at working men's clubs, which is not something I'd imagine Pep Guardiola does a lot of up in Manchester.

These are people who love their football and keep the players in a job, so the players should give something back. So many players do, without fanfare, but most could do more. I would have liked my players to go into schools and teach football, like I did. It would have kept the players' feet on the ground and been so exciting for the kids. Even when I was a kid at the worst school in east London, Tottenham legend Les Allen used to come in and coach us. If it wasn't below Les, it shouldn't be below the players of today.

You read about footballers getting up to no good, but most of them are great lads to be fair. John Terry got so much stick during his career, and of course he made mistakes. But you only ever read about the bad stuff in the papers. I'm involved with a charity called the Dream Factory, which grants wishes to kids with life-threatening illnesses and severe disabilities. There was a boy with cancer who was a big Chelsea fan, so a lady rang me up and said, 'Harry, what can we do for Tommy?' So I rung John up, and he was straight on the phone to this boy for half an hour. He was amazing, and that wasn't the first time he'd done that. If you were in trouble, you'd want John on your side. But despite all the good stuff John did, he ended up caricatured as a bad person.

When I was manager at Portsmouth, I got to know a young boy called Tommy Prince, who lived close to the ground. One day, Tommy got a bang on the arm during a match. He had to come off and his dad told him to stop being a baby. But when it persisted and they took him to hospital, it turned out he'd been hit on a tumour. When they opened him up, he had cancer all over his body. I got to know him well, and every time I met him he seemed happy. I asked if there was anything I could get him, and he said he wanted a bulldog. So I took him and his mum to the place I bought my bulldogs and got him one. He called it Bubba, and they were inseparable for the last six months of Tommy's life. Bubba was on his bed when Tommy died on his 16th birthday.

I'm not looking for a pat on the back or a medal, I just think that anyone like me, who has been dealt a good hand in life, should give some of their winnings back to others. I'm not better than anyone else, and often the only thing that separates the haves and the have-nots in life is a little bit of luck.

4

JUNGLE BOOGIE

'I just felt right at home ...'

I thought they'd start slinging people out of the jungle after a couple of days, until someone told me that no one would be getting binned until after two weeks. I couldn't get my head around it. Why would anyone want to watch a load of people sat in the middle of the jungle doing nothing for a fortnight? But I suppose that's what people like to watch, famous people being normal.

I had a nightmare start. We were split into two teams, given a boat each and told to have a race across this lake. The other team's boat sunk after about ten yards and we ended up winning by miles. But when I got out, I was climbing up this steep, muddy bank when someone pushed me in the back and I felt my knee go crack.

I knew straightaway I'd done some damage, because that knee had been giving me bother since my playing days.

Sure enough, it went up like a balloon. The doc gave me ice and anti-inflammatories and after a few hours listening to the others talk about a load of stuff I didn't understand, I got my head down next to the fire. When I woke up the next morning, my eyes were bright red and stinging like anything, because smoke from the fire had been blowing right in my face all night. I also felt like I had the flu. So now I've got a dodgy knee, dodgy eyes and a dodgy head. I felt like I'd been beat up and started thinking I might have to leave.

We were told that whoever won the boat race would get the best camp, which meant the girls and James got the worst one. I don't even think they had beds in their camp. They were sleeping on the floor, so they had a really rough first few days. It's not like our camp was anything special, and I didn't even have anywhere to sit. My luxury item was a chair (there was no point in choosing a football, I wouldn't have been able to kick it, let alone run after it) but they wouldn't give it to me because we didn't win enough stars in the first trial. They didn't mess about in there, it was like prison. But after about three days, my knee started to ease up and I started to feel a bit more like myself.

Saying that, it turned out Sandra was right, there was no caravan serving up coffee and bacon sandwiches. It didn't matter how hungry we were, they didn't give us anything apart from rice and beans. And even if you did a trial and won some stars, the food they gave us as a reward was disgusting. I was looking at this emu and kangaroo and those bloody wallaby wings and thinking, 'I can't eat that rubbish.' A cheese roll would have done me. People have said to me since, 'I didn't know you were a fussy eater, Harry.' Are they taking the piss? I'm not a fussy eater! I just couldn't face eating bloody wallaby wings. And I won't be ordering emu from the butcher this Christmas.

To be fair, Nick knew how to maintain a fire and was a brilliant cook. You could have dropped Nick into the jungle with nothing but a penknife, left him on his own for a year and he would have survived. He's the sort of bloke who can make something out of anything that happens to be lying around. Which is handy, seeing as he presents a DIY show on TV.

Nick did his best, but there was no pepper or spices to go with the meat, so everything came out bland. I'm lucky that I'm not a big eater – I can go all day on a bacon sandwich – so it's not like I was starving. But I did go four days without eating and drop a stone in weight, which probably isn't healthy.

The more time I spent with my campmates, the more I got to like them. They were lovely people, every one of them. Different to me, but lovely. A few of my mates ended up losing a few quid, because they all had money on me being thrown out. Before I flew out, one of them said to me, 'You won't last a week. There'll be no one in there to talk about football or racing with and someone will wind you up and you'll end up having a ruck.' But that didn't happen, everyone just got on from the start. There wasn't one person I could say a bad word about. We all got on fantastic, and that's what made it for me.

At first, I think some of them thought I was having them on by pretending not to know what was going on. I had to do a trial with Emily, which involved identifying film quotes while they poured insects over our heads. Luckily, Emily was quite good at it. But they couldn't get their heads around the fact I'd never heard of *Toy Story*. Truth is, I haven't been to the pictures since taking the kids to see *Jaws* in 1975. Before that, I took Sandra to see *Doctor Zhivago* in Romford. That was 1966, a year before we got married. I bought her a *Doctor Zhivago* coat that Christmas, like the one Julie Christie wore. Is it still two and sixpence to go to the pictures? I wouldn't have a clue.

I spent hours chatting with James about my childhood in the East End. I also loved listening to my campmates singing around the fire. Fleur is obviously a great singer, because she'd finished second on *The X Factor*, and John appears in musicals. But Emily and Rita had lovely voices as well. I'd name a song and they'd sing it, and I could have listened to them all day. Fleur and Malique also tried to teach me a bit of street slang. Peng ting? I still can't work it out. As I said, if I said 'peng ting' to Sandra, she'd think I was going to do some painting and worry I'd taken leave of my senses. DIY isn't my thing.

They also had me flossing, which convinced me I'd made the right decision to turn down *Strictly*. I looked like the Tin Man after a fortnight in the rain. But I still don't know what grinding is. Just before I left the show, they said to me, 'Harry, what's the first thing you're going to do when you get out of the jungle?' I replied, 'Do a bit of grinding with Sandra.' The next time I saw Sandra she said, 'Sorry, Harry, I've got a headache ... '

But there was also a lot of time sitting about doing nothing, and I'm not used to that. We weren't allowed watches and there wasn't a clock. It gets light very early in Australia, so I'd wake up in the morning at about five o'clock. Every day, me and James were first in the shower, which was freezing cold. It was just water running off some rocks, although it certainly sharpened you up. But then we'd have to sit there until ten o'clock, when they'd call someone to the Bush Telegraph hut. Inside the hut is just a wooden bench and a camera hidden in the wall, and someone behind the wall asking questions. After we'd had a chat, they'd give us a scroll and whoever it was would go back to the camp and read out a description of a trial. Two or three would go off and do the trial while the rest of us were sat round the fire, wasting the day away.

I didn't have a clue what was going on in the outside world. I'd ask them if Theresa May was still the Prime Minister or for the football scores and they wouldn't tell me. The only thing I did find out was the result of the Tyson Fury–Deontay Wilder boxing match.

I said to Lee, this cockney bloke, 'I was looking forward to the big fight between Fury and Wilder.'

'Do you want a bet on it?'

'Alright, I'll have a tenner with you. I'll have Tyson Fury.'

'Okay, Harry, I'll have the draw … '

I could tell by his face that the fight had already taken place. It cost me a tenner, but at least I found out who won. I never paid him anyway.

Straightaway I forgot that there were cameras in there watching us. They're hidden in bushes, behind rocks, and everything's camouflaged. There are cameras everywhere, and they're filming you 24 hours a day. When you leave the camp for a trial, all the security guards are in camouflage like the military, dressed up to look like trees, with branches coming out of their hair. So it never entered my head that there were millions of people sat at home watching our every move. As strange as it sounds, I just forgot we were on TV.

When I got out, Sandra said to me, 'You didn't half swear a lot.' That was because I just felt right at home. And compared to the girls, I was like a saint. Some of the stuff they were talking about after they went down to the creak to have a wash I can't repeat.

Those girls kept me entertained. Emily started asking me if my son Jamie was single, because I think she fancied a bit of him. I'll be honest, my initial thought was, 'No chance, you ain't got a prayer.' But when I saw her after we got out of the jungle and she was all scrubbed up, she looked very useful.

I said to her, 'Who are you?'

'Emily, I was in the jungle with you.'

'No you weren't, I've never seen you before ... '

There was no escape from the cameras in the jungle – there was even a camera in the shower. Another thing Sandra said to me afterwards was, 'You were having a shower with your pants on, washing your bum, you passed the soap to Fleur, and then she washed her face with it. I was sat there in the hotel watching it thinking, "Oh my God, what's he done? He'll never win it now!"'

Little did I know that the viewers loved seeing that sort of thing! Each to their own.

5
NOBODY'S MUG

'I'm a little bit more than a wheeler-dealer ...'

Never judge a book by its cover, because you'll jump to some pretty wild conclusions. For some reason, people seem to think I'm some sort of cockney wide boy who props up the bar at his local every night, chinning ten pints and boring people with the same old stories. But I've ever been much of a party animal.

I haven't had a proper drink in a pub for 40-odd years. And, believe it or not, I've never drunk a glass of beer. Even in my playing days, I only ever drank Bacardi and Coke. And I probably liked the Coke more than the Bacardi. Back then, people didn't really go down the pub with the aim to get legless. It was about having two or three drinks, listening to music and chatting.

Nowadays, I only drink with lunch or dinner, and even then it will be no more than a couple of glasses of wine. Away from football, I'm the exact opposite of my caricature. Me and Sandra lead a really quiet life. We aren't ones for going to dinner parties or restaurants in the West End. If we do get dragged up to London for whatever reason, we'll be the first to leave. And driving back to Poole with Sandra is the best part of the night. Most of the time it's just me and her, which is how we like it. I'm not close to many people down in Poole and it's not really a football hotbed, so nobody really gives me any grief. Me and Sandra are very private people who like each other's company, whether it's out walking the dogs or having a bit of dinner in a local restaurant. Give us a bit of pasta and a glass of wine and we're happy.

Sandra hates being in the limelight more than me. After I got out of the jungle and Piers Morgan asked us both to go on *Good Morning Britain*, she was mortified because we'd already been on *This Morning*. She said to me, 'Hazza, what have you done! I've already been on one show. Do I have to?' But Piers has been good to me over the years, so I managed to persuade her.

Even when I was still in football, I didn't mix with other people in the game. And functions and awards dinners were never really my scene. I always much preferred to be at home with the family. I don't really see any of my old West Ham team-mates. The only one I talk to regularly is Frank Lampard Sr, who was married to Sandra's sister. We did have a reunion a couple of years ago and it was a fantastic night. It was all the lads from the FA Youth Cup-winning team of 1963, organised by the guy who puts together the Hammers programme. He said to me, 'Do you see any of them?' And I said, 'No. But if you can get them all together, I'll book a restaurant in the West End and it's all on me.' Of course, some of them are no longer with us. And I hadn't seen some of the others for 50-odd years. It was strange seeing them all again, but it was a great, great night and very funny. Maybe we'll do it again in ten years' time.

A few years back, I did an interview that became quite famous. The bloke from Sky suggested I'd made my name as a 'wheeler-dealer', and I got upset and walked out. I thought that was a disrespectful thing for him to say. Some journalists were fair to me during my career, some weren't. Some of them understood what I was really like and stood up for me in their newspapers. But there were other journalists who didn't like me and were always looking to dig me out about something. One time, I did an interview for a magazine, and the journalist asked me if I'd ever been offered a 'present' to sign a player. I replied, 'I think every manager has, but I don't know of any who would take them.' I'd been in management for over 20 years at the time, so of course during that time someone had offered to look after me. That got twisted into 'Redknapp admits to being offered bungs.' What a liberty.

The media seem to be obsessed with this idea of me as a cockney barrow boy or Jack the Lad. There was a famous journalist who I'm convinced didn't like me simply because I didn't speak 'proper'. It gave me the hump, and it was all down to snobbery. They couldn't be more wrong about me. But I know who I am, and I'm happy with who I am. And that's all that really counts.

I think even the Football Association thought I was a bit rough around the edges, which is maybe why they appointed Roy Hodgson as England manager instead of me in 2012. I'd won the FA Cup with Portsmouth, taken Tottenham to the last eight of the Champions League and had been in charge of some of the best players in the world, including Gareth Bale and Luka Modrić. The public seemed to want me to be England manager, as did the press and the players. I got text messages from some of the lads in the team, including Steven Gerrard and Wayne Rooney. To be completely honest, I thought the job was mine. When the job came up, I'd just come out of a 15-day trial for tax evasion. And even though I was acquitted, I think the FA thought I was a bit of a risk. The FA look for a certain type of manager, and Roy fitted their mould. On reflection, I think putting on a suit every day and sitting in an office at FA HQ might have sent me crazy. I'm not really an office person and having to make speeches and give seminars is not really my scene.

It all comes down to the class system in this country. People make snap judgements and assumptions about someone purely based on the way they speak. People thought I was just a people person and a motivator, but with no clue about tactics. That's a load of cobblers. I played under Ron Greenwood at West Ham, who was years ahead of his time. I was coaching as a teenager, got my badges when I was 21 and have spent thousands of hours talking formations and tactics with some of the greatest minds in football.

When I was a kid, I'd sit in Cassettari's Café, just around the corner from Upton Park, and listen to Malcolm Allison, Dave Sexton, Noel Cantwell, Frank O'Farrell, John Bond and others talking in-depth about strategy. The tables would be cleared of food and tea and they'd start moving salt and pepper pots and sauce bottles around the table, pretending they were players. They were like generals in the army, planning a battle, and us kids would sit there enraptured. All those boys were great students of the game who went on to become successful managers, so there were no better teachers.

When Bobby Moore got his first management job, he wanted me as his assistant. This was a former England captain who'd seen me coach and obviously liked what he'd seen. So being called a 'wheeler-dealer' gave me the hump. It suggested that I was some kind of Arthur Daley character, blagging it as a football manager and taking shortcuts. No one knew more about the game than I did, it's just that the intellectualisation of tactics irritated me. Hardly anything is new, it's just that things get given new names, like 'tiki-taka' and 'Gegenpress', which just mean passing and pressurising.

I went to clubs and turned around their fortunes. When I took the manager's job at Bournemouth, they were in trouble. People said Bournemouth would never get out of the bottom two divisions because 'people in the town aren't interested in football'. But we won the old Third Division title in 1987, as well as knocking Man Utd out of the FA Cup a few years earlier. When I went to West Ham, they'd been a yo-yo team for years, up and down between the top two divisions. But in the seven years I was there, we never got relegated from the Premier League.

When I went to Portsmouth, they'd been flirting with relegation from Division One for four or five years. My mate rung me up and said, 'Portsmouth are 33–1 for promotion, I'm going to have a bet on them.' I replied, 'Keep your money in your pocket, if we can finish halfway, that will be a good result.' But we won the title in my first season. My mate wasn't too happy.

Tottenham were in trouble when I arrived, but I soon changed that as well, and we ended up in the Champions League for the first time and reached the quarter-finals.

And to make a difference at a struggling club, you have to go in, work out what surgery needs doing and change things. I've never met anybody clever enough to take over a bunch of useless players and turn them into a good team. So it meant offloading players who had been there too long and weren't good enough, and getting in players who were. That's not wheeler-dealing, that's just good management.

Nowadays, there are foreign managers everywhere, and people just assume they must be geniuses. But are they cleverer than English managers? Of course not, it's all nonsense. It's just that people hear a Spanish or Italian or German speaking English and automatically think they're more intelligent than someone with a cockney or Scouse accent. A manager's nationality has nothing to do with how good he is at the job. And certainly not how he speaks.

The 'big six' teams in the Premier League table have all got foreign managers, but they've also got the most money and the best players. And the reason they've got the best players is because they've got the most money. It's not rocket science. If you replaced Pep Guardiola with Burnley's Sean Dyche, Manchester City wouldn't suddenly drop out of the top six, they'd still be in the running for the title. My Sandra could take charge of that Man City team and they'd still have a chance. And if you put Guardiola in charge of Burnley, they'd still struggle, because the players aren't good enough. It's no different to horseracing: if you're a trainer and you get given a horse that cost peanuts, you're not going to beat the other trainer's horse that cost a load more.

Nowadays, everyone thinks they're a master football tactician, but you can argue about formations and tactics and systems until you are blue in the face, when football is mainly about the players. Bobby Moore said to me once: 'All those years I played under Ron Greenwood at West Ham and he never said well done.' I took what Bobby said on board. I had a go at players, especially during my early years in management, but it never made them play better. Even if someone has played badly, there's no point screaming and shouting at them. You've got to be more positive than that: 'Let's go again next week. You're good enough, so we will get a result.' You get more out of someone by telling them how good they are than by telling them what they can't do.

Whatever you do in life, if you're uptight, you're not going to be at your best, and footballers are the same. I loved a chairman coming up to me and saying, 'Harry, you're doing great, keep on going.' Whenever I joined a club as a manager, I'd often say to players, 'Hey, I tried to sign you when you were at Fulham,' and usually I'd get a positive reaction. And I'm sure players used to like it when I went up to them and said, 'You were different class today, absolutely fantastic.' When I was at Tottenham, I'd say to Luke Modrić, who was our best player anyway, 'Run the game and they won't get near you. You're too good for them.' It was all about giving him confidence, and it would make him feel ten-feet tall. We all love a pat on the back, there's nothing like it.

Talking up a player can also convince him to sign for you instead of someone else. Israel's Eyal Berkovic was all set to join Tottenham in 1997. They were considered to be a bigger club than West Ham, they were offering him more money and they had a large Jewish following. But when Eyal met Tottenham manager Gerry Francis, all Gerry was able to guarantee was that Eyal would be in his squad. So when it was my turn to speak to Eyal, I told him what he wanted to hear, namely that I was going to build the team around him. So he came to West Ham instead, and I did build a team around him.

Man-management is the ability to treat each player differently, depending on his personality. When I brought Paul Merson to Portsmouth, it was all about making him feel wanted and important. One time, he came to me and said, 'I've got a problem with the drinking and the gambling. Would you mind if I went and stayed at Tony Adams's clinic?' So I said, 'Not a problem, go and do what you have to do.' A few days later, I got a call from a friend of mine in Barbados. He'd just seen Merse walking down the road with his family. On the Monday, Merse returned to training with a lovely suntan. I said, 'Alright, Merse?' He said, 'Yes, gaffer, I feel a lot better.' Maybe I should have dug him out. But he trained brilliantly all week and scored both goals in a 2–0 win on the Saturday. Sometimes, saying nothing is the better option.

I might sound like Del Boy, but I'm a little bit more than a wheeler-dealer. And I'm certainly no mug when it comes to understanding people. Whether someone is from east London or Equatorial Guinea, the way you treat them as a manager is the most important thing. It doesn't matter if you're the manager of a football team or a call centre, treat someone with care and you will make them feel good and get the best out of them. And if you have the best players and they know their roles, they can play pretty much any way you want them to. All you have to do is let them know how good they are.

Graeme Souness once told me about his debut for Liverpool. He was sitting in the dressing room before the game and said to the manager, Bob Paisley, 'What do you want me to do?' And Bob replied, 'We didn't pay all that money to tell you what to do, but because we thought you already knew what to do.' Liverpool were the greatest team in the world, but there was nothing complicated about their philosophy. There's a lesson in that for everyone: just because something doesn't seem sophisticated, that doesn't mean it isn't.

6
EAST END BOY

*'The silliest little things can
make me smile ... '*

It's a completely different East End now to the place I grew up in. The docks have all gone and so have the dockers. West India Docks, where my dad used to work, closed in the 1980s and that's where Canary Wharf now is. A lot of my old haunts have long gone. There's not much singing in the pubs. On the rare occasions I go back there now, it's difficult to remember it as it was. And it was the East End as it was that made me. Like anyone, I'm a product of my environment, which is why the silliest little things can make me smile.

When I was growing up in the East End, nobody had a TV. During the day, my nan and all the other old girls would sit in the street, watching the world go by and chatting. That's how people kept themselves entertained in those days. It was a completely different world, and there seemed to be more community spirit than today. There was certainly less crime – we never used to lock our front door, even at night.

There used to be a pub on every corner in east London, but so many of them have shut. I lived right by a pub, the Cotton Arms, and I'd lay in bed at night listening to them all singing and dancing. The old girls and boys would still be singing when they poured out onto the street. I also remember the Queen's Coronation in 1953. We had a fantastic street party, with bunting and games. We still had rationing, so it's not as if it was lavish. But we had cake, and that was enough. People don't have street parties anymore, and the Cotton Arms is long gone, along with almost everything else I remember.

Those old cockneys were a different breed. My mate Tony's mum and dad have been married for 76 years and his mum was recently on the radio, talking about the war. One night, her and her family went down into the air-raid shelter and, when they came back up, their house had been flattened. So her and her family slept on the floor of St Anne's Church in Limehouse for three years. Imagine that, your whole street being destroyed during the night. When the interviewer asked why she wasn't evacuated, she said she couldn't go because she was sewing parachutes for the soldiers. Poplar was the first place to be bombed in London in the First World War, which not many people know about. My mum used to tell the story of her school suffering a direct hit, killing a load of kids. She remembered them all being laid out on the pavement.

I was watching the telly the other day and there was a piece about a lovely old man, who was part of the D-Day landings at Normandy and had just died. Imagine running onto that beach, the Germans firing machine guns at you and seeing your mates go down. It must have been like the fairground for those Germans. How do you have the guts to do that? Where were they running to? Did they even know what they were trying to do? Some of them didn't even make it as far as the beach, because they were loaded down with so much gear that they sank and drowned. I've been to the Arnhem Oosterbeek War Cemetery and when you stop and look at the graves, you realise that most of the people that died were just kids. It's just unreal when you think about it.

Me and Sandra have got a lovely house in Sandbanks, with a view over the sea, and we go on some lovely holidays. But we haven't always lived like that. When I was a boy, my holiday every year was hop-picking in Kent.

Hop-picking, or hopping, was what most working-class families from east London did of a summer, in the same way as people now might go on holiday to Benidorm or Tenerife. I first went when I was six months old, although I didn't do much picking then. Everybody on our street would jump on an old green lorry – or charabanc, as we called them in those days – and sing songs all the way to Kent. We'd be going through the Blackwall Tunnel and all the old girls would be singing: 'My old man said follow the van, and don't dilly dally on the way!' My mum and dad weren't really party people, but that would have been the closest thing to partying they did. They'd all have their legs up and be waving their arms about, because anywhere beyond the Blackwall Tunnel was like the Land of Oz.

When I look back now, hopping was probably harder than being in the jungle. We all stayed in a hopper hut, which had no gas or electricity but was lit by oil lamps. A tractor would come round the huts and someone would throw bundles of sticks, called faggots, onto the roof with a pitchfork. We'd make a fire with the faggots, sit around it and sing.

There were no restaurants about, although the adults would go to the pub at the weekend. While they were inside enjoying a couple of halves of mild, us kids would sit outside with a packet of crisps and a glass of lemonade. Back in the field, a bloke would come round at night, selling bread and cakes from a van. And we might club together with a couple of families in adjoining huts and cook a communal stew on the fire. We'd chuck in anything we had to hand, but the main cuts of meat would be rabbit or neck and scrag of lamb. But most of the time, we'd cook soup on a little Primus stove in our hut. Our beds were wooden pallets and mattresses stuffed with straw. You'd wake up in the morning – at six on the dot – with all this straw stuck up your bum.

My nan would be out all day picking hops, in rain or shine, and it was bloody hard work. When her bin or bushel was full, she'd call for the tally man and he'd come along and write it in his book. You'd get 10p a bushel, and she might earn 90p a day. But she'd still be getting subs of 50p a day to buy a bit of food or an ice cream for me. By the time she got home, she wouldn't have any money left. Kids today wouldn't be able to get their heads around going on holiday to work, but we had no concept of going abroad or staying in a hotel. Every year it would be the same families, so we all knew each other well and everybody loved it. It was the highlight of our year. You've got to remember, in east London, you woke up in the morning to birds coughing, so being in the countryside, breathing fresh air and seeing cows was a wondrous experience.

My first summer at West Ham as an apprentice, when I was 15, we were all supposed to go in and paint the crash barriers and the turnstiles, clean out the old Chicken Run stand and do other bits and pieces of maintenance around the ground. The problem was, I was supposed to go hopping, like any other summer.

Ernie Gregory, who was West Ham's former goalkeeper and now one of the coaches, was in charge of us apprentices. So I said to him, 'Ernie, I can't help out, I've got to go hopping in Kent.'

'What do you mean? You've gotta come in, you're supposed to be working.'

In the end, Ernie sent me off to see the manager. Mr Greenwood didn't know what hopping was, but he let me go for one last summer.

My mum and dad ended up buying a tiny little caravan down in Leysdown-on-Sea, on the Isle of Sheppey. We all used to go down on Friday evenings, after my mum and dad had knocked off work. We'd meet at Aberfeldy Street in Poplar, jump on one of the old green coaches with the plastic seats, and the journey in those days would take about four hours. We'd stop at a halfway house, everybody would go in for a cup of tea and a sandwich, and by the time we got to Nutts Farm it would be time for bed.

There wasn't a lot to do in Leysdown. There were a few arcades, and there was a bit of beach with some rocks on. But it was the seaside and there were fields, which was enough. Where we came from, we didn't know what fields were. I played games for Burdett Boys on Hackney Marshes, but our school matches took place on red cinder pitches. On Nutts Farm, there was a big field between the caravans and all the kids would play until it got dark. We'd have fish and chips for dinner and go to bed with big smiles on our faces. Then, on the Sunday, we'd get the coach back to London and arrive home at about eight.

I loved those breaks in Leysdown – it felt like the Seychelles to me. And when you're not used to much as a kid, you're likely to be grateful for anything nice that comes your way as an adult. Even today, I get excited by the smell of fish and chips. There's magic to be found in the simplest of things.

7
KING OF THE JUNGLE

*'Act normal, get on with it and
have a great time ...'*

When they put me and Noel in that 'palace' in the jungle, I didn't
think there would be a camera in there with us. So when I got out
and everyone was going on about him giving me a massage, I was
gobsmacked. I think people liked seeing two old fellas having a
laugh together. We might have been famous, but we're no different
to anyone sitting at home on the sofa watching us act daft.

Because I hadn't been drinking any water, I woke up in the
middle of the night with these terrible cramps. Usually when that
happens, I shout for Sandra. I used to scream so hard she'd think
I was getting excited about something. But on this occasion, Noel

was the only person about. So he got his hand under the bedclothes and started rubbing my leg. Then the other leg cramped up, so he started doing that one. When that happened, he must have thought I was having a wind-up. Then I got out of bed and started rubbing his feet. God knows how it looked on TV, two old blokes rubbing each other down in their pants. As I said to the campmates, I did tell Noel the cramp was in my calf and not my groin.

Me and Noel laughed ourselves to sleep that night, which was lovely. I just got on so well with him. When he came in late, he was made the camp Emperor, and he chose me as his advisor. That meant sleeping together in this palace, but I was honestly happier sleeping outside. This palace was full of insects and flies, because we had a light in there. And there must have been about a hundred spiders – big ones.

When we got in there, the first thing I said to Noel was, 'Are you only in here for one day?' I thought they'd brought him in for a guest appearance. But it turned out he was in permanently. I thought, 'That can't be right, we've all been here for five days.' But we ended up having a right giggle together.

I didn't know Noel, but I was on one of his shows many years ago. He used to have a feature called the Gotcha Oscars, where he'd play an elaborate practical joke on someone. One week, he did a Gotcha on the groundsman at Bournemouth Football Club, while I was the manager there.

This guy John turned up one morning to find all these blokes on the pitch. Obviously, he was confused and a bit angry, so he went up to them and said, 'Who the hell are you lot?'

'You've got moles on the pitch.'

'What do you mean, "got moles"?'

'Don't worry, we've got it under control … '

Suddenly, these explosions started going off all over the pitch and John was going mad. Anyway, a few weeks later, me and John had to go on the show. The problem was, Bournemouth had played at Bradford that afternoon and got beaten 1–0 in injury time. So they were driving me to the studio to go on live TV and I had the raving hump. During my chat with Noel, I said, 'To be honest with you, you were lucky to find John on the pitch at all.' I felt terrible afterwards, and I think John was a bit upset. But as I say, we'd just got beat.

While I was the oldest in there by miles, at least until Noel turned up, it's not as if I haven't spent a lot of time with people a lot younger than me. I'm used to being in dressing rooms and on coaches with young lads, so I know how they are, the stuff they like to talk about and how they behave. And I know a thing or two about team spirit. Team spirit is created through shared experiences. And that's what it was like in the jungle. It was boring at times, but it was often ridiculous. I mean, how much more ridiculous can you get than eating sheep's brains and fish eyes with Noel Edmonds, while dressed as Romans and shouting Yabba Dabba Doo? The answer is none more ridiculous.

People get the wrong idea about me, probably because of the way I speak. I wasn't a schoolteacher or an ogre as a manager, but I wasn't one of the lads either. It was different when I was a player. I was one of the chaps, a joker. If there were any pranks to be played, I was always in the middle of things. But once you become a manager, you're on your own. You can't mix socially with the players and you have to be serious, because you have to set an example. There's them and there's you, and that's the way it's got to be, because you can't let your guard down. So one of the great things about being in the jungle was being able to join in with the fun and not take everything too seriously. I could let myself go, because I didn't have to worry about what people thought of me. That night when Noel was massaging me, I was laughing my head off. In fact, I don't think I'd laughed that much in years.

*

SANDRA: *Harry would always be disappointed if he got beat as a player, but when he became a manager, he took defeats on board a lot more. Harry would be fine if his team won, but I could never arrange to go out with anyone on matchday, because if Harry's team got beat, he wasn't going to be a bundle of fun. Harry would be replaying everything in his head, while I just kept quiet and made sure I didn't mention the game. In the early days I used to say, 'Well, no one's died,' but you can only say that so many times. I did worry about him, but I knew he'd pull himself together and be himself again by Monday morning, when he had to go back to training.*

You've got to take the rough with the smooth in life, and Harry's job has meant we've had a great adventure. But just when I thought everything was quietening down, Harry got asked to go in the jungle. When he first told me he'd been approached, I sort of wanted him to do it. But I wasn't keen on the idea of him being away for that much time, and I knew that if he did well, I'd end up in the limelight, which

I really don't like. I also wasn't sure if he'd be able to cope with it all, which is why once he'd signed up for it, we decided it was best not to watch any old episodes, just in case he changed his mind.

I also worried that Harry might end up having a row with someone on TV, because he's a strong personality with a strong mind. If he doesn't like someone, he'll usually let them know about it. I was sitting in the hotel watching it with the other contestants' families thinking, 'Please don't say anything, Harry ... ' But it all turned out fine. In fact, I thought Harry had a chance of winning it after the first week. Obviously I was biased, but everyone kept on telling me how funny he was and how well he was doing. When Noel had one of those yabbies in his mouth and Harry went, 'Yabba Dabba Doo!' we were all falling about laughing in the hotel.

It was nice to see some of the old Harry. When he was still playing, he was always getting up to mischief. And he always found silly comedy funny, stuff like Benny Hill, Tommy Cooper, Norman Wisdom and Laurel and Hardy. But when he became a manager, he had to become very serious. Football managers have to keep everything in, they can't really let people know what kind of people they really are, because they have to appear strong. But I think most people just liked the fact that Harry came across as a normal fella ...

*

It was like being back in the dressing room as a player, except with people who had no interest in football. That was good for me, being around people for once who wanted to talk about other things. It was therapeutic, mind-cleansing. I can imagine it's a bit like going on a retreat or a detox break. Just being away from everyday luxuries was nice, sleeping outdoors and spending time with nature. I'm usually busy all day long, my phone does not stop going off, there's always someone asking me to do something. So it was really relaxing just lying back and listening to the noises of the jungle. Although how I went almost a month without having a bet is almost a miracle.

Sandra had told me that I'd have to eat a load of horrible things, like insects and grubs, and I was fine with that to be honest, it didn't really bother me. My knee never fully recovered, so I was just glad not to be running around. It also helps that I don't have any sense of smell, because I'm told some of those insects stink. It also made me the ideal candidate to clean out the dunny every day. I said to the others, 'Listen, cleaning the dunny out is not a problem for me, because I can't smell anything anyway. I'm no use with the cooking, so that can be my job – just call me Harry the shit-shoveller!'

The one Bushtucker Trial that I really didn't like was when they put me in a coffin with a load of rats. I hate rats, and when you get to my age, the last place you want to spend any time is in a coffin. I can't emphasise enough that that particular trial was not a bundle of fun. To try to take my mind off the situation I was in, I shut my eyes and thought about the nice meal and glass of wine I'd have with Sandra when I got out, and the sightseeing we'd do.

I do think some of the other guys had turned up to win it. They were fans of the programme and knew that winning it would do wonders for their careers. I've got no problem with that, because their business is showbusiness. Even the bit when it looked like me and Nick had a bit of a row wasn't really. We played this game where we had to drink five pints of nonsense and Nick ended up drinking three of his team's quota. I just thought it was silly, because he was his rugby club's beer-drinking champion, so what chance did anyone have of beating him? But it wasn't a proper argument, it was just a bit of fun.

It never occurred to me to play up to the cameras, because I didn't even know they were there. When you're a football manager, the last thing you're thinking about is playing up to the camera, unless you're Alan Pardew doing his little dance in the FA Cup final. I never thought about winning *I'm a Celebrity*. I'm not even a celebrity. It was enough for me that it was an adventure and a lot of fun, and I'd get to see a bit of Australia with Sandra and my granddaughter. Don't get me wrong, I didn't want to be the first one to get voted out, but finishing fourth or fifth would have been fine with me.

I couldn't believe it when Noel got voted out first. I was absolutely shocked. He liked his own space at times and enjoyed sitting on his own, on a bench away from the rest of us, almost like he was meditating. Actually, he nicked that bench off me, because that's where I liked getting away from it all too. But I also thought he was great entertainment and we got on like a house on fire. I honestly thought that Nick was going to win it, because I thought the show was about who could survive best in the jungle. Nick was cooking every night, looking after the fire, whittling and what not. Meanwhile, I couldn't do anything, apart from shovel shit. But obviously that didn't matter.

When Malique got voted out, John said to me, 'He hadn't been looking at the camera the last couple of days, he had his head down all the time.'

I said to John, 'Well, this is not an acting competition we're in.'

I suppose I shouldn't be too surprised I was crowned King of the Jungle, seeing as I've spent a lot of time in jungles during my life. The school I went to was a concrete jungle, without any shadow of a doubt. And the football world has got more snakes than a jungle, while some of the teams I managed had more lunatics than the school I went to, which is saying something.

But it wasn't like winning a football match, where you might know what you've done to win it. A couple of people have said I won it because I just got on with being myself. That was the real me, I wasn't trying to be anything different. At no point did I think, 'I'm on TV here, I should say this, that or the other to make myself look good.' I went in, acted normal, got on with it and had a great time. I took the mickey out of myself and laughed with everybody else. If you do that, people will either think you're an idiot or a down-to-earth bloke. Whatever the reasons, you've got to do new things when you start getting on a bit, because you realise you've only got so many days left.

I was working as a pundit on a game at Tranmere and people were screaming my name and clapping me as I walked up the touchline. Before the game, I was standing next to Steve McManaman, who's won two Champions League titles with Real Madrid, and there were all these people coming up to me and asking for selfies. It was mainly women and children. I must have done about 200 of them. Poor old Steve was standing there like a lemon. He thought it was hilarious, but I felt terrible and found it a bit embarrassing. I thought to myself, 'There's something wrong here!' Some well-known people get upset with people coming up to them all the time, asking for autographs and selfies. But as I say, it doesn't cost me anything to stop and have a chat.

When I went on *Good Morning Britain*, Piers Morgan told me I'd become a sex symbol. If there are any girls out there who find me sexy, they need their heads testing. Someone else called me a national treasure. I'm not having that, but it's certainly been different since I came out of the jungle. I'm not going to change just because I won *I'm a Celebrity*, but I've loved every minute of it. In fact, it's one of the best things that's happened to me. And if there was a lesson in me winning, it's that people enjoy their 'celebrities' to be down to earth and just like them. And that there's life in a lot of old dogs yet.

8
FINDING LOVE

'Maybe Sandra got a decent deal ... '

I met Sandra in a pub in Stratford in May 1964. One Sunday, my old mate Colin Mackleworth said to me, 'Fancy going up the Two Puddings? They've got a dance on.' We'd only just signed professional with West Ham, so were only 17. Anyway, we paid our ten bob to go in, went upstairs and there was a disc jockey playing Motown. I saw these two lovely girls dancing around their handbags and said to Macca, 'Shall we ask them to dance?' You never know when the love of your life is going to walk into your life.

Macca was a good-looking geezer, so I imagine Sandra saw us walking over and thought, 'I hope I don't end up with the ugly one.' But we got chatting and I asked if I could have her phone number. I still remember that number now: 01–594–1254. Macca ended up as an undertaker, so maybe Sandra got a decent deal . . .

*

SANDRA: *I remember I was wearing a pink shift dress that night. And while Harry might not remember his chat-up line, I do. He said, 'I'm on the telly on Wednesday.' He'd played in the England team that won the youth European Championship, and they were getting an award on* Sports Personality of the Year. *I thought, 'What a show-off.' I didn't even know who West Ham were, because my dad wasn't interested in football and my brother was more interested in rugby.*

People sometimes ask me, 'What did you like about Harry when you first met him?' The truthful answer is, 'Not a lot!' It certainly wasn't love at first sight. But I obviously liked him just enough to give him my number, which I wrote in pink lipstick on a scrap of paper. Maybe a week later, one of the girls I worked with at the hairdresser's said to me, 'I heard Harry Redknapp took you home. Did you know he's ginger?' I honestly didn't think he was, because it was quite dark in the Two Puddings . . .

*

Sandra was the first girl I'd ever gone out with. For our first date we went to the Lion and Lamb in Brentwood, Essex. I asked one of my team-mates where was good to eat, and they recommended there. Today, Brentwood is famous for *The Only Way is Essex*, but back then it felt like the countryside for someone from the East End. If I remember rightly, we had scampi and chips. A few weeks later, Frank Lampard Sr came into training and said, 'Harry, I took a girl home last night called Pat. You're seeing her sister.' Frank had met Pat in the Ship in Stepney, so it was complete coincidence.

Me and Sandra would occasionally go to parties, but we were always pretty quiet. Mostly, I'd pick her up on a Saturday night after work and we'd go out for dinner, just the two of us. The West End wasn't really our scene, we'd have felt a bit out of our depth up there. So we'd have a bit of dinner in the Moby Dick in Chadwell Heath, or the Dick Turpin in Newbury Park. When I joined West Ham, I learned what a prawn cocktail was, so I used to eat them all the time.

It's not as if girls in those days went out hunting for footballers. Sandra and Pat had no idea who we were, and neither did their dad. Like my dad, Bill Harris worked down the docks. He was a foreman and had arms thicker than my legs. Bill was a lovely fella, but me and Frank were scared stiff of him. And Brian, their brother, was just as big, so we were scared stiff of him as well.

Because Sandra came from Barking, which in those days was considered Essex, I thought she was posh. Her mum and dad owned their own house with a little garden. It was only a semi-detached, but I'd come out of an old block of flats in the East End, so I thought it was a palace. We didn't even have a phone. If I wanted to call Sandra, I'd have to go down to the phone box at the end of the road with a pocketful of pennies and have a chat while someone might be pacing up and down outside, giving you dirty looks. If it was somebody who looked a bit tough, you'd wind the conversation up sharpish. And even though Sandra's house had a phone, it was on a 'party line', which was used by everybody on her street. You'd pick up her phone and hear her neighbour talking.

When I took Sandra home after a night out, Bill would start banging on the bedroom floor if I stayed longer than ten minutes. It was the same for Frank when he took Pat home. Bill would be thumping away and I'd think, 'Bloody 'ell, I think it's time to go!' Sandra's mum, who was the loveliest woman, was a bit worried that I liked a punt, because gambling had been the downfall of her dad. Bill once went off alarming at me because he'd found out I'd been to the dogs: 'I don't want you messing around with my daughter if you're going to waste your money gambling!' But they got over it in the end, and when I asked Bill if I could marry his daughter, he said yes ...

*

SANDRA: *I can't remember the moment I thought, 'I really like this guy.' We didn't catch up for a couple of months, and Harry was quiet around me at first. When my friend told me her dad had told her that Harry was always mucking around, I said, 'I think you've got the wrong bloke.' But after we'd been out a few times, I realised he was funny, a bit of a prankster.*

Harry's team-mate Roger Cross had been seeing my best friend Joy for a couple of years, and then Frank started seeing my sister Pat, but it was all a complete coincidence. We certainly weren't WAGs. On holiday one summer, Harry and Frank Lampard Sr would spend all day showing off on the beach, doing keepy-uppies, bouncing the ball off their shoulders and heads. But that didn't really impress us.

I never watched Harry play the whole time he was at West Ham, because I was always hairdressing on Saturdays. Women didn't really go to football in those days anyway. My sister Pat worked there with me, and there were three other sisters, including my boss. All five of us worked in the same hairdresser's until we got married and had children, and we absolutely loved it. I used to put the commentary on in the hairdresser's and one week, when West Ham were playing Leeds, Harry had a bit of a barney and got sent off. I was very embarrassed.

Another reason we weren't too bothered about our boyfriends being footballers was because they didn't make a lot of money in those days. And my mum didn't like it that Harry used to go to the dogs and gamble, because her dad was a gambler, and was worried Harry might go the same way. But my mum and dad realised what a nice person Harry was in the end.

Harry's mum was one of the loveliest people I'd ever met. We never had a cross word in all the years we knew each other. She was so funny. She was quite dry and would come out with one-liners that would make you laugh, like Harry on I'm a Celebrity. *But she was so shy. If Harry said someone was coming round, she'd go all blotchy. The flat was always lovely and clean, but I think she was a bit embarrassed about where she lived.*

I was the first girl Harry took home, and I loved his mum to bits. His dad was lovely as well, although a bit cantankerous and obstinate. Sometimes I look at Harry and think, 'Oh my God, he's turning into his dad.' Harry's more like his mum, but he's got a lot in common with his dad, because he had a heart of gold as well ...

*

We got married in 1967, at St Margaret's Church, Barking. After that, we had a little do at the Loxford Social Club in Ilford, where Sandra's dad was a member. It was just a room with a little bar and a bit of music, nothing too grand, and a few villains from Canning Town turned up. Don't worry, I invited them. Frank Lampard Sr was supposed to be my best man but he broke his leg playing against Sheffield United and ended up on crutches. We've got a photo somewhere of Frank with his leg up and me signing his plaster.

When I told my dad I was thinking about buying a house, he thought I'd gone mad: 'You can get a council house, why are you wasting your money?' He had no concept of owning a property, and he never wanted to leave the East End. When I moved to the south coast, I tried to get them to move down with me, but they wouldn't have it. My mum and dad moved from the Burdett Estate to a flat around the corner on Rhodeswell Road and stayed in the East End all their lives. It was the only life they knew and the only life they wanted to know. But me and Sandra did end up buying a lovely semi-detached in Cavendish Gardens, Barking, for £6,200. It was about ten minutes from Sandra's mum and dad's, had central heating, a nice little garden and was absolutely perfect for a newly married young couple.

The modern footballer might go to the Seychelles or Bali for his honeymoon, but me and Sandra went to Torquay. I'd just bought a car off John Bond, who was one of the senior players at West Ham when I first joined. I'd come out of the café with Frank, and Bondy was parked up in this lovely red S-Type Jaguar. Bondy saw me admiring it and said, 'Do you want to buy it?' I said, 'I can't afford that,' but he suggested I take it for a spin. This Jag had a wooden steering wheel, a wooden dashboard, spoke wheels, and drove like a dream. When I got back after a couple of circuits of East Ham High Street, Bondy said I could have it for 250 quid. I sold my little Morris 1100, took delivery of the Jag and was absolutely over the moon.

Anyway, me and Sandra set off for Torquay in style, but on the way down there the head gasket went. We had to stop every 20 minutes because it was overheating and it took eight hours to get there. It gets worse. Bondy was playing for Torquay at the time, so the owner of the hotel we were staying in said, 'Oh, I know John, bring him over for dinner one night as our guest.' So me and Sandra had this slap-up meal and a few bottles of Liebfraumilch with John, his wife Jan and their kids, as well as another former West Ham player called Billy Kitchener and his wife. When they gave me the bill, I explained that the hotel owner had invited us over, only for the waiter to tell me the owner had gone away on holiday for two months. So I copped the bill, got cleaned out and couldn't afford to get the Jag repaired.

The drive home took even longer than the drive down. As you can imagine, Sandra wasn't best pleased. Neither was I, especially when I took a look at the log book and discovered the Jag was two years older than Bondy had told me it was. But me and Sandra weren't going to let a little thing like a dodgy motor come between us. It was a case of for better for worse, for richer for poorer, in sickness and in health, to love and to cherish, till death us do part.

9
JUMPERS FOR GOALPOSTS

'We were footballers, not celebrities ... '

If I had the choice between playing now and back in the day, I'd choose back in the day, every time. We didn't earn a lot of money, and we lived similar lives to the man on the street, but we had the best of times.

Impossible as it is to imagine now, when the Premier League is like the League of Nations, me and most of the other lads at West Ham came from within a few miles of Upton Park. I came from Poplar, Bobby Moore and Trevor Brooking were from Barking, Frank Lampard Sr was from East Ham, Martin Peters was from Plaistow, and so on and so on. John Bond lived in a terraced house 100 yards from the ground. Geoff Hurst was about as exotic as it got, and he was from Chelmsford. When we signed Bobby Ferguson, who was Scottish, it was like we'd signed someone from outer space.

We were all mates, from the time we were kids. We played football with or against each other at school. A lot of our dads worked on the docks together. We were steeped in the history and culture of the club, because a lot of the players had been fans, stood on the terraces with their dads and come through the youth team together. If you're reading this and can remember playing football with all your best mates at school, that's what it was like playing for West Ham in the 1960s. Now, I couldn't even tell you who half the players at West Ham are. They turn up, spend a season kissing the badge and sign for someone else as soon as they get the chance. A lot of them have no understanding of the football club or the fans, and no interest in learning.

The Friday before a game, we'd all go to the dogs at West Ham Stadium – not to be confused with the football stadium. It wouldn't be a late one, but we'd all be there, having fun together. If it was an away game, we all used to play cards on the coach and have a laugh and a chat. Loads of the lads were punters. Johnny 'Budgie' Byrne, so-called because he didn't stop chattering, would always turn up to training with the *Sporting Life* under his arm, wander out with a mug of tea and sit on a bench studying the form for 45 minutes.

There was a time when we didn't even have a club coach. We had an old minibus that was painted claret and blue, and if we went round a bend too quick, you might end up with a load of boots and Bobby Moore falling on top of you.

Now, players don't even speak to each other. You see them getting off the coach and walking into the ground wearing these giant headphones. Apparently, they're 'getting into the zone'. I have to laugh. When I played, the players did everything together. After a game at Upton Park, we'd be in the Black Lion in Plaistow before the fans had got out of the ground. Wallop, everyone in the pub. The whole team would be in there, win or lose. We never missed a Saturday night, even if we'd been hammered 5–0. Even then we wouldn't get any bother, because everyone in the Black Lion was a mate.

We were footballers in those days, not celebrities. As I like to say, we were East End boys, not West End boys. The Black Lion had been there for about 500 years, and Milly, the old girl behind the bar, had been there almost as long. There would be music and Vi, the landlady, would put on a lovely spread, with roast beef sandwiches, bowls of jellied eels, cockles and whelks.

The only player in the 1960s who was considered to be a celebrity was George Best. The rest of us could walk into any pub in London without anyone noticing. Even Bobby Moore could go drinking in the Baker's Arms in Stratford and no one would bother him. Bobby wasn't really one for drinking champagne in flash nightclubs, he was far more at home hanging around with his mates in the East End, drinking in pubs that footballers nowadays wouldn't be seen dead in. Can you imagine Raheem Sterling and Sergio Agüero piling into a pub round the corner from the Etihad after a game at Man City? Don't be silly. Now, Premier League players can't leave the house without being recognised, asked for selfies or abused. I don't envy them that.

Incredible as it sounds, the day after a game on a Saturday, we'd often have a kickabout over the park with our mates. It would be jumpers for goalposts, and Bobby Moore, captain of England, would be playing against lads who could barely run or kick a ball.

Afterwards, we'd all head to the pub, or maybe back to Bobby's house for a party.

But some of us did like to make ourselves scarce after getting a bad beating. We got slaughtered 6–1 by Man Utd at home in 1967, which was the day they clinched the Division One title. Bobby Charlton ran rings around us, George Best scored, Denis Law got a couple and Colin Mackleworth, my old mate from Burdett Boys and the fella I was with when I met Sandra, was in goal. So that night, me, Sandra, Colin and his girlfriend drove as far into the countryside as we could go so that we wouldn't be seen. Colin never played for West Ham again, which tells you how brutal football was back then, and still is.

Football in England hadn't moved on much by the time I'd started managing in the early 1980s. The day after Bournemouth knocked Man Utd out of the FA Cup in 1984, one of the TV channels asked if they could come down to the training ground and do some interviews. I had to tell them we didn't have a training ground. We trained at King's Park, which was public land. Before we trained, the apprentices had to go around picking up dog mess.

In 1986, we had back-to-back games against York and Darlington. The directors were never going to put us up in a hotel, but it seemed silly to drive all the way back from York to Bournemouth only to drive straight back up to Darlington. So I found some cheap guesthouses in York and hired a couple of minibuses and a skip for the kit. We trained for the first game at York Racecourse and we when turned up at Darlington, the bloke on the gate thought we were supporters. He couldn't get his head around the fact that the Bournemouth team had made the trip up in a couple of clapped-out minibuses and the driver was the manager. We lost the first game 2–0 but after winning the second game 3–0, we sang all the way home to Bournemouth.

The Monday after we beat Man Utd, we trained on the park's cinder pitch, because the grass ones were too boggy. It was a great session, everyone was buzzing from two days earlier, but when we went to leave, there was a padlock on the gate. The park keeper had come round and locked us in, without bothering to tell us. We had to climb over a ten-foot fence to get out. I remember being at the top, swaying from side to side, and all the lads falling about laughing. Whenever someone kicked a ball over the fence, we'd have all the players searching the bushes until they found it, because we only had a dozen of them. Nowadays, players boot balls all over the place and nobody cares less. Truth be told, lower league football then was more like park football is now.

The Premier League and the clubs will argue that one of the reasons fans pay more nowadays is because the product is better than it used to be. Okay, players are fitter and quicker than they used to be, and they eat better food and drink less alcohol, but they don't have more ability with a football than players in the top league in my day. Those players learnt to play in the streets from the age of four or five. They had mastered a football – or tennis ball – by the time they were teenagers. Their basic skills were amazing. Some of the people I played with and against were incredible footballers: Bobby Moore, George Best, Bobby Charlton, Dave Mackay, Jimmy Greaves, who was an absolute genius.

Football was more aggressive and physical back then, no doubt about it. Broken legs would finish careers in those days, yet players would fly into tackles with abandon, week after week. And that style of football didn't really change until the advent of the Premier League in 1992 and the subsequent influx of foreign players. And if you did get injured, your physio – or 'sponge man' – would jog on the pitch and squirt some water on your leg.

I recently watched the 1970 FA Cup final replay between Chelsea and Leeds, and it was a really vicious game. If it had been played today, there would have been something like 18 yellow cards and 6 reds. But that was just part of the game in those days, and even players who kicked people could play.

My favourite team from the 1960s was Don Revie's Leeds. No doubt, they had an even harder edge than most teams. When I played against them for West Ham in 1968, I got sent off, despite the fact I was beaten up by about ten of their players. While they were all stood around punching me, Bobby Moore and the rest of my lads were standing watching. And as I walked off, Mooro just shrugged. But that Leeds side was perfectly balanced. Norman 'Bite Yer Legs' Hunter could sort people out when he needed to, but he also had a left foot like a magic wand. Billy Bremner and Johnny Giles could also dish it out in midfield – despite both of them being only little – but they were also amazing footballers. Eddie Gray was a genius dribbler, Peter Lorimer had a dynamite shot and Allan 'Sniffer' Clarke would score for fun up front.

Believe it or not, Southampton were more dangerous than Leeds at that time. After beating Liverpool in 1970, Liverpool's manager Billy Shankly called them 'alehouse footballers'. Southampton could actually play some football, but Shankly had a point. In that game, John McGrath, Southampton's centre-half, kicked Alun Evans in the throat. And here's another funny story that tells you how hard that Southampton team was: Jimmy Gabriel, who I played with in Seattle, told me that he once had a fancy-dress party round his house and Denis Hollywood, Southampton's Scottish left-back, came as a schoolboy. While Denis was cycling home that night, wearing his blazer, shorts and little cap – like the lead singer of AC/DC – someone cut him up. So Denis caught this car up at the lights and dragged this bloke onto the street. The poor fella must have thought the schools in Southampton were out of control.

The main difference back when I played was the boots we wore, the weight of the balls we used and the pitches we played on. When I was managing Tottenham, Gareth Bale would receive a new box of boots every week. He had hundreds of them. But when I played, I had two pairs of boots: a pair with moulded studs and a pair with screw-ins. Even Bobby Moore didn't have a boot deal. If he wanted to change them for a better pair, he'd have to go to Arthur Sedgwick's sports shop in Walthamstow and pay the difference. Your boots would be hung up on a peg in this dingy old boot room and if you had a pair you liked, you stuck with them. You might have the same pair for three years. If they split, you'd get Jack the kitman to take them to the cobblers and get a leather patch sewn over the top.

Here's a story that tells you just how heavy those old leather balls were: when I was playing for West Ham against Wolves in 1970, the referee was knocked spark out by a Bobby Moore clearance that hit him flush in the face. While he was laid out in the penalty box, everyone just played on without him. All except for Bobby, who strolled over to the ref, picked up his whistle and blew it as hard as he could. The game came to a halt and the ref regained his senses. That was the power of Mooro!

Pitches are better now at the end of the season than they were at the start of the season in the 1960s and '70s. Up until the 1990s, most pitches in the country were ankle-deep in mud by October. At West Ham, a band used to play on the pitch, about 30 blokes stomping their feet, churning up the grass. Nobody ever told them not to go on there, and they did it for years. It was the same at Arsenal, a band marching up and down the pitch before kick-off and all through half-time.

Now, you can't even set foot on the pitch. I was doing some punditry at Chelsea a couple of years ago with Gianfranco Zola, one of the club's greatest players, and Gianfranco was standing with one of his shoes over the touchline. One of the groundsmen tapped him on the shoulder and told him to get off.

While it's easy for people to laugh at how mollycoddled modern footballers are, the way players were treated in the past was often appalling. Nat Lofthouse was at Bolton Wanderers for over 20 years and scored more than 250 goals for them. After he retired from playing, he became a coach at the club. One of the coaches' jobs was to clean the ground on Fridays, and one day Nat complained to the manager that he was getting shit on his hands while cleaning the toilets. The manager was very embarrassed and apologetic, and the following Monday he handed Nat a pair of rubber gloves and a longer brush. Nat Lofthouse scored more top-flight goals than Wayne Rooney.

We did our best for our clubs for as long as we could, but once we were done, nobody really gave a shit about us. Look at Bobby Moore: he played over 500 games for West Ham, was a special player, a fantastic captain and a great guy. Every kid in the country wanted to be Bobby Moore. But when he left, he wasn't welcome at the club in any shape or form. He even got thrown out once for not having a ticket.

People are often afraid of past players with big names and don't want them hanging around. But if they'd had any brains, they would have made Bobby an ambassador for club and country, like Franz Beckenbauer in Germany. He should have been sat in the front row of the director's box whenever he wanted, the face of West Ham. If they wanted to sign a talented kid, he should have been sent round the kid's house to meet the parents. That might have been the difference between the kid signing for West Ham or Arsenal. Instead, we have people who know nothing about football running clubs and the FA, simply because they've put some money into the game. These people have no idea about football. They certainly don't know more about the game than Bobby Moore did.

After Bobby died, they built statues and named stands after him, plastered pictures of him all over Upton Park. But while he was alive, they didn't want to know him. Once, I took West Ham to play Grimsby. I looked up and saw Bobby sitting at the back of the stand, doing radio punditry for a hundred quid on a freezing cold night, eating fish and chips out of a bag. This was one of the greatest players who ever lived. That was football. And, for most people, that was life, and still is. That said, being a footballer was a wonderful life back then. Everything is shinier now, but that doesn't mean everything is better.

10
LESSONS IN LOVE

'I wonder if I love Sandra too much ... '

My son Jamie always says to me, 'Dad, how did you pull Mum? You were punching so far above your weight it's unbelievable. You won the lottery meeting her.' He's not wrong. But there's no magic formula. From that first day I met Sandra in the Two Puddings, I've loved her to bits, and I'm sure she's loved me. And 55 years later, we're still going strong.

I always say that the whole time I was managing football teams, Sandra was managing me. I'm useless at most things, no use around the house at all. I can't change a plug and struggle to boil an egg. How many minutes is it? Three? Ten? I just guess. Sandra likes her eggs scrambled anyway. She treats me like a baby: packs my bags for me when I go away, gets my washbag ready, folds up my socks and pants and handkerchiefs. And she's like her dad, can do anything around the house, whether it's changing bulbs or replacing fuses.

Nick taught me how to wash up in the jungle – Sandra always tells me I leave the cups the wrong way up on the draining board – and if the telly ever switches itself off, I'll start shouting: 'San, the telly's gone off! Make it come back on again!'

It's so important for any manager to have a supportive wife, although I never wanted Sandra involved in football. You'd see a lot of wives in managers' offices after games, pouring the drinks and fussing about, but Sandra hardly ever came. I certainly didn't want her coming and watching when things were going badly and fans were giving me stick. She would rather have been at home anyway. I'd come home after a game and we'd go to a little Italian restaurant and have a couple of glasses of wine, just the two of us.

I travelled a lot as a manager. When I was at West Ham and Tottenham, I was still living in Poole. I'd be up at four o'clock and on the road by five, to make sure I missed the traffic. I'd sometimes stay in a hotel a couple of nights a week to break the week up, but I didn't like being away from home. So when I could, I'd drive back again. If we'd just had a game and we'd lost, I wouldn't be a bundle of fun. And Sandra was the only person who could make me feel better. She put up with a lot, but never put any pressure on me to stop.

Me and Sandra have hardly been apart since we met, because we just love being in each other's company. When I went on tour to America with West Ham, I was away for seven weeks. Back then, you didn't phone home, you wrote each other letters, about the most everyday stuff. I remember Sandra sending me a letter telling me our dog had finally barked. We thought he had no barker inside him, so she was really excited. And I was reading the letter and saying to the boys, 'Amazing! The dog's finally gone and barked!'

We've never even had an argument, because you couldn't have a row with Sandra if you tried. If I get upset about something she'll say, 'Look at you, calm down.' She's so placid and easy-going – she's always worrying about other people and never says a bad word about anybody. She could be a Samaritan.

Not that it's been all plain-sailing. Sandra's had five years of illness and it's been a nightmare. First, she broke her kneecap falling over the bloody hoover. She took a couple of painkillers, crawled up the stairs and went to bed. When she woke up in the morning, she was in agony and had to call an ambulance. Not long after that, she found out the nerves in her neck were touching and she had to wear a cage. We went on holiday to Portugal and she didn't feel too good, and it turned out one of the screws had fallen out. The specialist said that if it had gone down her windpipe, it could have killed her.

I've already mentioned the sepsis, and then there was the time I ran her over. I parked the car on this little one-way street, Sandra got out and I thought she'd crossed the road. Meanwhile, I was thinking, 'I'm taking two spaces here, I better move back a bit.' But unbeknown to me, Sandra hadn't crossed the road at all and was still standing next to my back wheel. As I reversed, I went right over her ankle and sliced it in half, like a rasher of bacon.

I jumped out of the car to find Sandra laid out on the floor with a lady holding her head. She said to me, 'Don't look at her foot,' but I did and I immediately thought she was going to lose it. It was absolutely horrendous. She had to have plastic surgery – they took some skin from her hip. She never blamed me, just said it was one of those things. I suppose it was, but I certainly felt guilty about it. That was a real blow, really difficult to live with.

The only downside to spending your life with somebody you love to bits is that you start to worry how you'd cope if anything happened. When Sandra's sister Pat died in 2008, it was a sobering moment for all of us. They were so close, every day they'd be on the phone to each other for ages. Pat was fit as a fiddle and then, out of the blue, she was gone. It was the same with Sandra's mum. Her dad was downstairs, making some tea, and her mum was upstairs packing to go on holiday. Bill called out, 'Your tea's getting cold!' When he got no answer, he went upstairs and found her on the floor. She'd had a brain haemorrhage and was only 51. By the time we got to the hospital in Romford, she was gone.

I've seen it happen to other couples: one partner goes and suddenly life for the other one becomes very difficult. After my mum died, my dad struggled terribly. He'd catch a bus to the cemetery in Wanstead every day, because he had nothing else to do. My mum had done everything for him, so he couldn't cook a thing. He'd eat pie and mash for lunch and fish and chips every night for dinner. He was a lost soul, and it was difficult to see him like that.

When you hit your 70s, those things enter your mind for the first time. I wouldn't have a clue what to do without Sandra's support. I try not to think about it too much because it scares me. I sometimes wonder if I love Sandra too much. If anything was to happen to her, it would kill me.

When I was in the jungle, they called me into the Bush Telegraph and the girl inside said, 'Harry, you've got to leave the camp now.'

'Why? Am I doing a trial?'

'No, just do what I tell you. There will be a producer there to meet you.'

My heart sank. I thought they were going to tell me something bad had happened to Sandra, because a lot of bad things have happened to her lately. But when I got out, Sandra was there. I couldn't believe it, I was thrilled.

Before I went in, somebody said to me, 'Do you think you'll cry in the jungle?' Cry in the jungle? Don't be silly. Why would I cry in the jungle? We did one trial where we only won seven stars, which meant that only seven people would get a letter from home. I was quite happy to be left out, so I said to Noel, 'As long as the girls all get one, I'm not fussed.' When Noel got his letter, he started crying. I thought, 'Hang on, this is a bit much. There are blokes in the army, who don't see their loved ones for months on end, and we've only been in here a couple of weeks.' But when I saw Sandra, I was as bad as any of them, maybe worse. There I was, sobbing my heart out. People have told me they cried as well when they saw it on TV.

*

SANDRA: *Harry's always been quite old-school and had a stiff upper lip. Men certainly didn't cry in Harry's day and he doesn't really talk about his feelings. So I found it strange when he was talking about our relationship like he did, and I was shocked at how emotional he got when I turned up. A lot of married men would probably love to get away from their wives for a month, but I think a lot of young people saw how Harry reacted and thought, 'Wouldn't it be lovely to have a relationship like that?' We've been lucky, because we've always just got on.*

Harry can be romantic. One Christmas he said, 'I didn't know what to buy you.' But when we went to bed, there was a present under my pillow, which turned out to be a bracelet. And two Christmases ago, he put a ring in a cracker. For a few seconds I was thinking, 'Wow, these must be expensive crackers . . . ' But when we were on This Morning *and they asked for five relationship tips, I could only think of three: going out together, talking (although Harry is on his phone half the time, so people probably think we don't) and never going to bed on an argument. That's worked for us.*

We rarely have an argument and if we do, it's finished in ten minutes. I don't like confrontation, it stresses me out. Harry is more fiery than me, so if I was to start going back at him, it could end up in a big row. So if Harry upsets me, I'll tell him the following day. Otherwise, I might say things I wish I hadn't said. People say some horrible things during the heat of an argument and then regret it. And all my life, I've never wanted to have regrets, because regrets play on your mind.

I think it would be fair to describe me as Harry's manager. Not just his manager, I'm his electrician, his plumber and pretty much anything else. Harry can just about make toast and boil an egg, but he's never cooked a meal. He always hangs his clothes up, but he makes a mess of everything else. When he has a shave, there's water all over the bathroom. If he has a shower, he blocks the plughole. He'll spill orange juice all over the worktop and floor in the kitchen, usually the day after the place has been cleaned. And he hasn't got any better since he came out of the jungle. He still leaves the cups the wrong way up on the draining board.

I'll see the mess he leaves and think, 'Mr Pastry's been at it again.' Mr Pastry was a character who used to be on TV years ago and was always doing things wrong, a bit like a black-and-white Frank Spencer. If Mr Pastry was doing wallpapering, he'd get off the ladder and put his foot in the bucket of paste. That's Harry. Another time, I was looking out of the window and Harry was washing the car with one of those jet cleaners. Next thing I know, Harry's turned the jet cleaner on the flowers and taken all the heads off. He said to me, 'I thought I was far enough away that the water would just drop on them.'

I thought Harry might struggle with retirement. I'd say to him a lot, 'Are you playing golf today, Harry?' But he keeps himself very busy, is always on the go. In fact, although he's stopped managing, he's not really retired. I like to keep myself fit and see my own friends, because it's nice to have different interests. But we go out together a few times a week, and Harry loves seeing the grandkids, going to the races and walking the dogs. It made me laugh when I went in the jungle and the first thing Harry said was, 'How's the dogs?' I thought, 'Harry, you really should be asking about the grandchildren!'

I think a lot of couples give up on relationships too easily. But me and Harry have never even been on the point of giving up. If you asked me what the most important thing in Harry's life was, I'd say me. And vice versa. I do sometimes think about how my life would have turned out if we hadn't gone to the Two Puddings that night, more so the older I get. I look at people who have had a tough life and it almost makes me feel guilty because I've been so blessed. Harry's got older since I met him, but who hasn't? Other than that, he hasn't changed at all. He's a kind, caring person and I've always known how much he loves me. He's my life, and every day is a good day with Harry.

*

Since I've been out of the jungle, everyone wants to know the secret of a long-lasting relationship. It's difficult for me to put my finger on, because I just happened to meet somebody I loved. And that just happened to be in a boozer in Stratford. My mum and dad were married all their lives, as were Sandra's, and I do think that people back then tried harder to keep things together. But you don't know what goes on behind closed doors. If I'd married an ugly old bird sitting there with her rollers in, or someone I didn't stop arguing with for ten years, it might have been different and I might have ended up getting a divorce. But I married a super-fit bird who I get on great with.

My life with Sandra is fantastic. We're solid as a rock and every moment I spend with her is precious. I was lucky to have met her. There ain't no secret.

11
CIGARETTES AND ALCOHOL

*'Spaghetti isn't going to help you
kick a ball straight ... '*

The manager wasn't too happy with all the boozing that went on when I was playing. Even back then, it wasn't a great look for a team to get beat and then get legless on the train back from Manchester. But the main perk of being paid not much money is that you can get away with being a little less professional.

One night we played Stoke away and were absolutely terrible. Ron Greenwood was furious and wouldn't let us leave the hotel. But a few of us climbed out of the window and headed to a nightclub in town. When we got back to the hotel, the gate was locked, so we had no choice but to climb over the top. Unfortunately, Bobby slipped and caught his foot on a spike. He told Ron he'd had a gardening accident and didn't play for two weeks.

Nowadays, there would have been pictures of us trying to get Bobby off that spike all over the internet in minutes. Trying to lead a normal life is a lot more difficult for players today. Everyone knows who they are, everyone has a camera on their phone and everyone wants a selfie. And nowadays, a player can't even have a puff on a fag without it making the front page of a newspaper.

One Christmas Eve, we were all in a pub called the Globe in Stepney when a load of girls from a local factory turned up. Suddenly, the barman was shouting at Bobby, telling him his wife Tina was on the phone. Bobby was supposed to be taking her out and she'd been ringing around all his local haunts, trying to track him down. Bobby promised her he'd be home right away, which we all knew was nonsense, and half an hour later Tina rang again. Bobby made more promises, had another drink, and Tina phoned for a third time. This time she said she was going to phone Bobby's mum. Bob was laughing about it with the lads when the door swung open, like in a Wild West film, and Bobby's mum marched in with the raving needle. She grabbed Bob's arm and dragged him towards the door, as if he was a naughty schoolboy, not the World Cup-winning captain of England. And just before they left, she turned and said, 'One of you has been mixing his drinks, because he doesn't get drunk like this!' The last thing we heard was, 'But Mum, I'm 29!'

As well as the England football team, Bobby could have captained an England drinking team. Bobby's motto was 'win or lose, on the booze'. There was even afternoon drinking after training, which increased after Jimmy Greaves arrived at the club in 1970. Jimmy's mate owned a pub down the road from the training ground, and we'd all be in there until the evening. The landlord would get drunk, take himself off to bed and we'd serve ourselves.

When we were on a train, travelling back to London after a game, Bobby would buy up every drop of beer in the buffet car. Ten minutes from Euston, he'd disappear into the toilet, have a shave, put a new shirt on and reappear looking immaculate, before heading out on the town. Bobby was a great trainer – he'd always come in on Sunday morning, put a bin bag with armholes cut out of it under his tracksuit, do a dozen laps of the pitch and sweat out the booze – but he was always one of the chaps and never wanted to miss a night out.

Bobby used to tell the story about the night they won the World Cup. They didn't really know where to go, so they ended up at Danny La Rue's nightclub in the West End. When the chaps turned up, the place didn't have a free table, so they had to wait outside until one became free. Eventually, the manager came out and led them to a table right next to the toilet.

We didn't even have a gym at West Ham, just a small room where we'd play head-tennis. One year, we had a lot of snow, which meant we simply couldn't train on the training pitches for six weeks. The manager found a sports hall in Harlow, so we'd drive there in a minibus and play four-a-side matches. And we were one of the most forward-thinking clubs in the country. Some players from that era didn't even train with a ball. They spent every day running round a track instead, the thinking being that if they didn't see a ball all week, they'd be foaming at the mouth to get hold of it on a Saturday.

We never ate at Upton Park or the training ground, because neither of them had canteens. We might have got a cup of tea if we were lucky. For breakfast, I'd have an egg and bacon sandwich on the way in. And for lunch, we'd get four-bob dinner vouchers to use at the Central Café, round the corner from the training ground. Or, if we were at Upton Park, we'd go up to the aforementioned Cassettari's. There was no chicken and pasta for players in those days, it was more like steak and kidney pie, boiled potatoes and peas, or a spot of ham, egg and chips, with jam roly-poly for afters. And then we'd all roll back in for the afternoon session. It's a wonder we could stand up, let alone run around. Billy Bonds used to put away steak and chips, half a loaf of bread and butter and rice pudding a couple of hours before a game. Remarkably, there wasn't an ounce of fat on him. Before setting off after an away match up north, we'd phone ahead for fish and chips and pick it up a couple of hours later.

Nowadays, every training ground has chefs and the canteens are like top-class restaurants. They'll have eggs however you want them for breakfast, and at lunch they'll have a menu with a choice of half-a-dozen dishes. But eating right doesn't make you a good footballer. Of course, it's good to have nutritionists and dieticians and everything else, but no amount of spaghetti is going to help you kick a ball straight.

Food was also bit easier to understand when I was younger. When I did *This Morning* with Phillip Schofield and Holly Willoughby, the chef Phil Vickery made jam roly-poly and custard, pie and mash and jellied eels. Phillip Schofield had never tried a jellied eel and actually quite liked it, albeit with a bit of vinegar. But I used to absolutely love them. One night, I fancied a bowl of eels, so stopped off at Tubby Isaac's stall in Aldgate.

I said to him, 'A nice bowl of eels please, Tubby.'

'Of course. What's the time?'

'Nine o'clock.'

'Can you mind the stall for me for ten minutes?'

Next thing I know, Tubby's running towards Aldgate East tube station. So I'm standing there all flustered, and two black cabs pull up. I said to these fellas, 'Tubby's gone, 'e'll be about ten minutes.'

'Oh, right. George, what you 'avin'?'

And this bloke started helping himself to two great big bowls of eels.

'There you go, George. Few more?'

I thought it was a set-up, like *Candid Camera* or something. I didn't know what to do, I was just stood there staring at them. I wasn't going to say anything, so in the end I jumped in my car and left them to it. Where I live now, they don't even know what jellied eels or pie and mash are. Don't get me wrong, I like a nice Italian. But if you've never tried jellied eels, you haven't lived.

When I went back to West Ham as manager, the boozing was completely out of control, way worse than when I was there as a player. I soon banned them drinking in the players' bar, which upset a few of them. But they'd smuggle booze onto the bus, pass around vodka and brandy mixed up with Coke in plastic bottles. They'd all be eating crisps and chocolate bars and the odd one would be smoking. They were like a bunch of teenagers. One night, we went down to play Dorchester Town in a testimonial, but when it was time to leave the hotel and drive to the ground, a few of the players were missing. They finally turned up about half an hour before kick-off, fall-down drunk.

Another time, we all went for a day out at Cheltenham Racecourse. On the coach down, I was reading one of the broadsheet newspapers, and there was an article in there about our striker Lee Chapman and his love of wine. Chappy was a northerner but, for some reason, was always quite posh.

I said to him, 'I didn't realise you were a wine expert?'

And he said, 'Oh yes, boss, I've always been interested in wine.'

When we got down there, I was in this private tent with all the players, who were a bunch of lunatics, and I bought a bottle of cheap champagne and a bottle of Dom Pérignon. I asked a waitress for two towels, wrapped them up, gathered the lads around and said, 'Chappy, I'm going to test your skill. Let's see if you can tell an expensive champagne from a cheap one.'

'Oh, boss, it's so easy. I don't even have to taste them, I can tell just by looking at the bubbles.'

Anyway, Chappy tasted them, guessed wrong and the lads absolutely slaughtered him. I liked Chappy and we normally got on well, but on that particular occasion he got the hump and started accusing me of switching the labels.

Alex Ferguson loved his wine as well. After Portsmouth played Man Utd in the FA Cup one year, he invited me and my assistant Jim Smith into a private suite and brought out a £600 bottle. We couldn't really stretch to that at Portsmouth – you might get a miniature bottle of Blue Nun if you were lucky. Not that I know

Sir Humphrey Gilbert was the worst secondary school in the East End. We turned up late, caused mayhem, got the cane and went home again.

Hop-picking was what most working-class families from east London did of a summer, in the same way as people now might go on holiday to Benidorm or Tenerife.

My mum and dad were good people. I grew up poor, but they made sure I grew up happy.

The Two Puddings, Stratford, where I met Sandra. On the rare occasions
I go back to the East End now, it's difficult to remember it as it was.

Me and Sandra got married in 1967, at St Margaret's Church, Barking.
It was the best thing I ever did.

Me, Sandra, Mark and our first family dog, Matty. Back in those days, a footballer's front room looked much like yours.

Sandra has been there for me through the highs and lows of football management, even when my choice of leisurewear plumbed the very depths.

Me and Sandra have hardly been apart since we met, because we just love being in each other's company. The whole time I was managing, she was managing me.

Me and my dad with my boys Mark and Jamie. My dad was football mad and still making Jamie sandwiches when he was playing for Liverpool.

West Ham, 1964. The blokes in the caps include 1966 World Cup winners Bobby Moore, Geoff Hurst and Martin Peters.

As a football-loving kid growing up in East London in the 1960s, the only club you wanted to play for was West Ham United.

Football was very different when I was playing. In fact, turning out for a First Division team in the 1960s would have had more in common with modern non-league. And the wash woman was probably the only female around.

Football management was very different back in the day – can you imagine Pep Guardiola collecting balls at the end of a training session?

In 1990, I almost lost my life in a traffic accident during the World Cup in Italy. At least I got an award out of it – and a couple of glasses of champagne.

With former England striker Luther Blissett at Bournemouth. Players of Luther's class were hard to come by outside the top division, but it was a lot of fun.

Having been appointed assistant manager to my old teammate Billy Bonds, I was given the top job in 1994.

Football management is intense – here's me as Portsmouth manager in 2003, during a victory over Leeds. Leeds were relegated that year.

much about wine. We must have about 300 bottles in the house and we never drink it, because we just don't unless we're eating.

When me and Sandra went on *This Morning*, we had to be at the studio quite early, so went up to London the day before. We booked a nice restaurant and because the waiter thought I could afford it, he gave me the dearest wine on the menu. And that's not the only time I've been tucked up with wine. I'm a fearless spender, love a bet and am generous beyond belief, but I'm not a wine connoisseur. In fact, I can't tell one bottle of wine from another. So sometimes I'll choose the cheapest on the menu. In fact, I did it the other night, a nice glass of Argentinian Merlot. Who cares if the waiter thinks I'm mean? It's the same with food. Someone will say, 'You've got to go to this restaurant, it's absolutely amazing,' but when you go there the food's a load of crap. I can only imagine people convince themselves that certain restaurants are amazing because they cost a bloody fortune. However much it costs, it's not a patch on jellied eels.

Ron Greenwood had a reputation as one of the most forward-thinking coaches in the country, but some of the training back then was so basic. The first day of pre-season, we'd get on the scales, get weighed and that was it. There was no testing for fat percentages or body mass index or anything like that. Then we'd all jump on a coach – first team, reserves, youth team – and head to Epping Forest for some running. Nobody would bother stretching, we'd climb straight off the bus and head off in our plimsolls. And we wouldn't just run through the forest, we'd run down the Epping New Road in single file, with cars and lorries flying past at 80mph. Brian Dear would often hitch a lift on a milk float, before jumping off a few hundred yards from the finish. We'd do that day after day for ten days, and sometimes we'd bump into Tottenham players doing the same. Then we'd head back to the training ground, have our massive lunches, before doing ball work for 90 minutes, our guts full of food.

The worst state I saw a player in at pre-season training was John Hartson, when I was manager at West Ham. John was 36lb overweight and couldn't run. I told Frank Lampard Sr to stick him in a wetsuit, take him over the woods and get him running. John couldn't even keep up with Frank, and he was in his 50s. He ran 300 yards before having to sit down on a log.

While things weren't as scientific in those days, I did used to keep a note of players' weights in little black book. One day, I had a go at Ian Bishop for being out of shape. He wouldn't have it, so I went and fished my little black book from the boot of my car and discovered that he was two stone too heavy. Now, every club has about ten fitness coaches, which means that a manager can let them get on with that side of things and concentrate on coaching the football.

When I first started out in management with Bournemouth, my backroom staff consisted of a fella called John Kirk, who we inevitably nicknamed 'Captain'. John was my assistant, kitman, laundry man and physio. By the end of my management career, my backroom staff might consist of 20 or 30 people. We'd have goalkeeping coaches, a doctor, a psychologist, sports scientists, fitness coaches, masseurs, nutritionists, a chef, computer analysts and two or three media people. On any given matchday, a random punter could have walked into our dressing room wearing a club tracksuit and nobody would have known if he was supposed to be there or not.

My physio at West Ham was a guy called Bill Jenkins, who wouldn't treat you on a Sunday unless you brought him a bottle of wine or half-a-dozen lagers. Bill was one of the scariest men I've ever met, and the reason we had so many injury problems was because nobody ever wanted to be treated by him. He'd put these sucker pads all over you and turn his machine up as high as possible so that it felt like you were being burned alive. And if he had been drinking, he'd be even more sadistic. His son Rob took over from him and although he was nicer than his dad, he'd be treating you while eating a bacon and egg roll, so that brown sauce would be dripping all over your legs.

Physios weren't really physios in those days, they were usually just old players who'd been promoted from groundsman. If you got injured during a game, they'd run on the pitch and rub a wet sponge over the affected area, before telling you to get on with it. Newcastle had a physio called Charlie Mitten who was a big greyhound racing fan, which meant the players often couldn't get on the treatment table because he'd be rubbing one of his dogs down instead.

At Bournemouth, we had a lovely old boy called Arthur Cunliffe, who played a couple of times for England. One minute, Arthur was doing a few odd jobs around the club, the next he was our physio. When I arrived at Bournemouth, they'd just got a new ultrasound machine. So when I tore a muscle, Arthur used this machine on me for three days. On the fourth day, there was still no improvement, so I thought I'd make myself busy and take a closer look. 'Arthur,' I said, 'I don't think this machine is switched on. I think a little light is supposed to appear.' He'd been using that machine on all the injured players since pre-season. No wonder nobody was getting any better.

Football is a lot more complicated today, that's for sure. But how many modern players could tell you a story about being treated for an injury by a machine that wasn't switched on? As I say, things are a lot more professional nowadays. But there's no way footballers have as much fun as we did. Who wants to be eating chicken and pasta for lunch every day? Live a little.

12

ALWAYS GRAFTING

'Work hard at whatever it is you do ...'

When I managed Bournemouth, I might watch my team play on Saturday, Newport County on Sunday, Plymouth Argyle on Monday, Enfield on Tuesday, York City on Wednesday and Carlisle United on Thursday. Any night there was a game on, I'd be there, trying to pick up players and learn a thing or two. Being a football manager has changed, but one aspect has stayed the same: if you want to be successful at it, you've got to work all the hours God sends.

My main message to kids is, work hard at whatever it is you do. You've got to work hard to get anywhere, especially in football. I've seen kids come into football clubs with big reputations, schoolboy internationals who think they've already made it. But all they're interested in is the big house, the expensive watch and the expensive car with all the trimmings. They're already in the comfort zone, have lost any hunger they ever had, and they end up nowhere. But I've seen other kids come in with far less ability who practise and train their hearts out, because they're desperate to become a footballer.

Hard work isn't a magic wand, but it can be a recipe for success. I like to tell kids about Alan Ball. When Bally was a kid at Bolton, the manager called him into his office and said, 'Listen, son, the only apprenticeship you're going to get is as a jockey.' Bally was devastated. But when he got home, his dad said, 'Don't give up, son. Prove them wrong.' Bally never got much bigger, but he practised so hard he ended up winning the World Cup with England.

Frank Lampard Jr was the best trainer I saw. The only other person I saw who came close was his dad. They were a million miles ahead of anyone else. Ron Greenwood was going to let Frank Sr go to Torquay when he was about 17, but Frank wasn't interested in leaving West Ham. He said to Ron, 'What's wrong with me?' Ron said, 'You're not quick enough,' because Frank Sr couldn't run. So Frank Sr went out and bought some spikes and every day after training, he'd practise sprinting over ten yards. People back then thought it was impossible to become quicker. But every day, Frank Sr got quicker and quicker and quicker. Frank Sr played more than 500 games for West Ham, leaving 20 years after Ron wanted to flog him. And his kid's work ethic was the same.

I'd be at the training ground at Chadwell Heath, it would be raining and getting dark, and I'd look out of my office window and see Frank Jr doing his sprints, just like his dad did 30 years earlier.

He'd take a bag of balls and a couple of cones out, swerve past the cone and shoot from 25 yards – Left foot, bang! Right foot, bang! – and after using up all the balls, he'd go and collect them, bring them back and do it all over again. He'd do that every day for an hour, without fail.

One day I was talking to the groundsman and he said to me, 'Someone's climbed over the fence from the school next door.'

And I said, 'No, it's only young Frank.'

When a player is as committed as Frank was, other players buy into it because they see it produces results on a Saturday. Another kid who was football through and through and always hungry to learn was Rio Ferdinand. He'd fire questions at me about football for hour after hour.

When I was a kid at West Ham, we'd stay after training and carry on playing football on the forecourt. One day, the coach Ernie Gregory, who was a great player and servant of the club, turned up and said, 'Come on you lot, ain't you got homes to go to? I've got to lock up.' The manager found out and said to us, 'If you want to be out there playing football until eight o'clock at night, I'll make sure someone's there to keep the place open.'

Ron could see the bigger picture. As far as he was concerned, we were doing something useful with our time, instead of getting up to mischief. And all that practice was making us better players. And all the great footballers I knew became great footballers because they trained and practised more than most.

But nowadays, clubs have rules dictating how much training kids can do a day. It's madness telling kids not to practise. Whoever came up with that rule can't possibly have been a football person.

The other day, someone told me that they took a kid out to do some extra crossing practice and another coach came out and said, 'What are you doing?'

My mate said, 'He's working on his crossing. It's no good.'

And this coach replied, 'He did crossing practice this morning, he can't do any more.' So my mate had to take this kid in.

If Frank Jr was a kid today, someone would no doubt have told him he risked shortening his career through overtraining. It's scary to think what might have happened to Frank Jr if he'd had coaches like that, preventing him from spending hours on his own, when everyone else had gone home, learning his craft. He might not have made it. What actually happened is that Frank played more than 600 games and was one of the best footballers this country has ever produced.

But for every Frank Lampard, Jr and Sr, there are a hundred talented young footballers who simply don't have the determination to fulfil their potential. I had Adrian Randall at Bournemouth and he was a tremendous player. He was big and strong, great on the ball and glided over the pitch. He seemed to have everything. But he never made it because he lacked the one thing anyone successful footballer needs: drive. Adrian was just too laidback. I wanted to shake him sometimes, because I'd never seen anyone as talented.

One of the most talented kids I ever saw was Ravel Morrison. I remember speaking to Alex Ferguson about him. Alex said, 'We've got a kid at Man Utd who is the best 12-year-old I've seen in my life.' Alex had never seen anything like it – he was talking about Ravel like he was from another planet. But then he said, 'The kid has issues ... '

About five years later, I took a team to Old Trafford and said to Alex, 'Whatever happened to that kid you were telling me about, the best you'd ever seen?'

'Oh, he's still here. We're struggling to keep him on the straight and narrow.'

I ended up taking Ravel to QPR and he was an incredible talent. My God, he could ghost past defenders and do unbelievable things with a football. But the last I heard he was playing for some club I'd never heard of in Sweden. It didn't help that he had people in his ear telling him he was bigger and better than he was. When I had him at QPR, his agent Barry Silkman was constantly telling me Ravel was better than Gareth Bale, yet he couldn't even get in my team and Bale had just played in the Champions League final for Real Madrid. Was Ravel more talented than Frank Lampard Jr? Of course. Will he achieve one-tenth of what Frank achieved in football? Of course not.

But it's not just the case that talented kids don't fulfil their potential because they can't be bothered. Footballers have personal problems like everyone else. You don't know what's going on at home. Their parents might not get on, they might have had a kid at a very young age, they might have got in with a bad crowd. I did worry about what some of these young kids might be up to when they weren't at the training ground. And I always thought I could change them. But some of them were already too far gone, didn't like the discipline or conformity required to make it and were impossible to control. They usually didn't last long. If a kid was a genius, like Ravel Morrison, you'd persevere. He was a harmless kid really, a nice enough lad, but he'd been around the wrong people for too long and picked up too many bad habits.

Then there are the kids who just don't like straying too far from home. When I was manager at West Ham, I signed a kid called Joey Beauchamp from Oxford United. When he turned up, the first thing he said to me was, 'I should have gone to Swindon.'

'No, Joey, Swindon is the opposite direction on the M4.'

'No, I should have gone to Swindon.'

'Nah, you wouldn't go to Swindon to get to West Ham ... '

I thought he was saying he'd gone the wrong way. What he was actually saying was that he should have signed for Swindon instead of West Ham. Apparently, West Ham was too far from where he lived, and the traffic was terrible. Joey was a fantastic footballer, but he just didn't want to be in London. Joey never played for me. We sold him to Swindon. He could have thrived in the Premier League, but he didn't want it. It's a very simple lesson.

13
PARENTHOOD

'Manners cost you nothing ...'

I always wanted kids, but I was useless at some of the hands-on stuff. I've got to hold my hands up, I've never changed a nappy in my life. Sandra wouldn't have trusted me anyway. I'd have made a right mess of it, put it on back to front or something. Like Mr Pastry. But I wasn't the only dad in those days who didn't change nappies or stroll about with a baby in a sling. That's just not what dads were expected to do. That's my excuse. But as long as a mum and dad know their roles and are happy with them, that's all that matters.

Where was I when my first son Mark was born? You know what, this is terrible, but I can't remember for sure. *Sandra?!* I'm pretty sure I was nowhere near the hospital and, if I had to guess, I was probably playing football. In those days, footballers didn't have a day off just because their wife was having a baby. If you'd suggested it to your manager, he would have laughed you out of his office. You played a game, jumped in the car afterwards, drove to the hospital and hoped the baby had been born before you arrived. I was there when Jamie was born, in the hospital, but not in the room. I was sat outside in the corridor, like Del Boy in that episode of *Only Fools and Horses*.

Sandra would have loved a little girl as well, but we had two boys and called it a day. And as soon as we had the boys, her life was mapped out for her: football, football, football. It never gave Sandra the hump, she just got on with it. Mind you, it's almost impossible to give Sandra the hump, and I'm sure there are plenty of women who don't like being married to footballers, despite the nice life it gives them.

I might not have changed their nappies, but I took Mark and Jamie everywhere with me. When I was training with Bournemouth, Mark would come along. And when we went over to America, when Jamie was just a couple of years old, they'd both be on the touchline.

It was important to me and Sandra that the boys had good manners and spoke to people properly, because that doesn't cost you anything. They knew they had to be respectful and they were, whether it was to their nans and granddads, who they were both very close to, or waiters and waitresses in restaurants. If they didn't speak right to their mum or whoever else, I'd let them know about it. It's the same with my grandkids now. I'll say to them, 'Don't talk to your mother like that.' Or if someone puts some food in front of them in a restaurant and they carry on staring at their phone, I'll tell them to put their phone away and say thank you. I wasn't a disciplinarian, but I could be strict, although I don't remember Sandra ever having to say, 'Just you wait until your dad gets home!' Any parent needs to instil discipline into their kids.

We were lucky in that Mark and Jamie were both good kids, never gave us much trouble. Although we did end up in court with Mark once, when he was ten. Him and his little mate wanted to go over the park to play football, so I said to them, 'You're not to go on the road with your bikes. The road's dangerous, ride them on the pavement.' So they were riding on the pavement and this policewoman came past and nicked them. Looking back, it was unreal. It was the quietest pavement you've ever seen. We ended up in court in Christchurch – it was the most bizarre situation. The two of them ended up behind bars for six months. Not really, they just got a ticking off. But I obviously had the raving needle about it.

Mark and Jamie both had paper rounds when they were little. One morning, Jamie overslept, so I went out and helped him. I was manager of Bournemouth at the time. At this one house, I was pushing a paper through a letterbox when the door opened to reveal this old fella standing there in his dressing gown. He'd obviously been standing there for ages, waiting for his paper to arrive so he could read it with his breakfast. So he said to me, 'What time do you call this?'

'Sorry, mate, got held up.'

'Is that you, Harry?'

'Yeah, that's me.'

'I'm a season ticket holder at Bournemouth. What you doing delivering the papers?'

'They don't pay me much, I need to supplement me wages ... '

We'd always sit round the table for dinner and Sandra would cook a roast every Sunday. A lot of families don't do that nowadays, they all eat dinner in front of the TV at different times. When I played in America for Seattle Sounders, we were out as a family almost every night, whether it was for hamburgers, fish and chips or pizza. And when we weren't eating in restaurants, we'd have barbecues down by the lake with all my team-mates and their families.

Bobby Moore and his wife Tina would be there, Geoff Hurst and his wife Judith. There was also former Tottenham and Wales defender Mike England and a few great Scottish lads, Jimmy Robertson, Jocky Scott and Gordon Wallace. The wives and kids would get the barbecue going and when we finished training, we'd join them. We'd have a swim and some food and sit by the lake until nine o'clock every night. Then we'd pack up and all head back to the apartment block where we all lived. It was like paradise, especially for a load of lads from east London and working-class towns in Scotland.

Mark and Jamie were both okay at school, but football took over their lives at a young age. As early as I can remember, they were kicking footballs about, and as long as they were playing football or doing athletics or pretty much any sport, they were happy. I don't even remember them bringing girlfriends home as kids, that's how into their football and sport they were. Mark was a good athlete, a champion 100m runner and a good footballer. He played right-back, was quick, strong and a good passer. But he didn't have Jamie's raw talent. I knew Jamie was going to make it from the age of about five.

When Jamie was six, he was playing for the under-tens where we lived in Christchurch. In fact, he got thrown out of the league because someone told them how old he was. How silly can you get? I can understand it when there's some kid with five o'clock shadow and a beer belly running rings round a load of ten-year-olds, but when he's four years too young? Madness. Jamie could have been better than okay academically, but he was training over at Tottenham from the age of 11. When I was manager at Bournemouth, sometimes I'd take him to school and he'd say, 'Can I come training with you instead?' And I'd say, 'Go on then, but don't tell your mum.' I'd bring him home at four o'clock and pretend I'd just picked him up from school. As Sandra sometimes says, he couldn't add up very well, but he got bloody good at football. I just knew he was going to be a footballer, and a very good one.

When I moved on to coaching the Seattle Sounders, we had a game against George Best's team, Los Angeles Aztecs, and lost 5–4. We had this young, inexperienced goalkeeper and he had a nightmare. The goals went in under his body, through his arms and between his legs. The following morning, this goalkeeper was on the treatment table and Jamie, who must have only been about four at the time, went up to him and said, 'Gee, Cliff, you really blew it yesterday.' I was mortified. Cliff probably was as well. I told Jamie to shut up and clear off, and he replied, 'But he did blow it, Dad!'

Even as a little kid, Jamie could volley the ball and had fantastic technique. He was never without a football. I think he slept with a football. When he was about four, we were having a kickabout and Mike England was in goal. Jamie said to Mike, 'I'm gonna put it in that corner.' Mike said, 'You mustn't tell me where you're gonna put it.' And Jamie said, 'No, I'm gonna put it that corner.' And Jamie stepped up and put it in the other corner. I'll never forget that. I saw Mike a few years ago and we laughed about it.

I was never one of those dads who stood on the touchline shouting and hollering. I never said anything or interfered, I used to just stand right out of the way and watch the game in peace. I might have suggested a couple of things in the car on the way home, but I didn't mention the game once we got indoors, let alone criticise how they'd played. It was all about just letting them enjoy it. I watch my grandkids play now and I'll stand by the corner, miles from all the parents, because I don't want to hear what they have to say.

It makes me cringe when you hear all the silly things parents shout from the touchline. I watched a game the other week. These poor kids were trying to have a bit of fun on a Sunday morning and their dads were screaming at them. This one kid looked like he was being moved about by remote control. His dad was shouting at him, 'Get here! Go there! No! Not there, here!' This kid must have only been nine years old and he was panic-stricken. He probably got a bollocking when he got home for not listening. I felt like saying to the dad, 'Why don't you just let the boy play football? You're ruining his enjoyment.' The kid was no good anyway, he was never going to be a footballer, so just let him have fun. The thing is, I'm sure his dad was no good at football either.

When I was at West Ham as a kid, no one was allowed to shout from the touchline. The only people who were allowed to shout at the kids were the coaches. They were Ron Greenwood's rules. If any parents piped up, one of the coaches would go up to them and say, 'Excuse me, we don't have any of that here.' That's how it was, and if they didn't like it, they were asked to leave. The whole philosophy was just letting the kids have fun and express themselves.

It's the stupid things they shout that get me. I was watching an academy game recently and there was one little kid, who must have been about 11, doing fantastic things with the ball. I was standing there thinking, 'Oh my God, look at him. How's he done that?' He was dragging the ball back, doing stepovers and every other trick in the book. I could have stood watching this kid all day. Suddenly, he got the ball again, tried something and lost it. And all the parents started shouting, 'Get rid of it! Don't be so greedy!' All because he hadn't passed the ball to their kid. It was the first time he'd lost it in the 15 minutes I'd been watching him. Can you imagine someone shouting at Lionel Messi when he was 11 or 12: 'Oi! Lionel, you greedy bastard! Stick it in Row Z!' It's scary how thick some people can be. My message to kids is, 'Keep dribbling. Learn how to dribble and you'll stand out, because no one can dribble anymore.' It's all pass, pass, pass – beating an opponent is a dying art.

There was one time I opened my mouth when I shouldn't have. I used to watch the games with my mate and his wife. We'd have a cup of tea, stroll up to the pitch and have a chat on the touchline. Their boy was playing in the same team as Mark, way out in the sticks somewhere, and the other side's manager was also the linesman. Anyway, this linesman kept shouting to his defenders, 'Run up! Run up!' and every time the defenders ran up, he'd put his flag up and shout, 'Offside!' This kept happening, even though our boys' side weren't offside most of the time.

Eventually, my mate said to me, 'Harry, was that offside?'

I said, 'Well, probably not, but I don't wanna get involved.'

Five minutes later, he said to me again, 'Harry, was that offside?' I said, 'Nah, it weren't offside, the geezer don't know the rules.'

So my mate shouted at the linesman, 'You can stick that flag up your arse!'

The linesman replied, 'I'll stick it up your arse in a minute, mate.'

With that, he marched up to the linesman and give him a right-hander – BOSH! I still didn't get involved.

Mind you, you hear about referees being attacked all the time now. They give up their time on a Saturday or Sunday morning and they shouldn't have to put up with being punched or abused or spat at. Give these people the respect they deserve. Even in professional football it's got beyond a joke. When I played, it was just banter. You might say something like, 'Come on ref, you're having a shocker!' And he'd look at you and reply, 'You're not playing too well yourself, Harry.' And that would be the end of it. I know it sounds very genteel, but I'd rather have that than a referee being abused and covered in spittle.

Both my boys played for me at Bournemouth, but Mark broke his ankle at 18, smashed it to pieces, and that was the end of him really. That was a difficult time for me, because I was the manager and the physio kept saying to me, 'He's got a low pain threshold.' So I kept saying to Mark, 'The physio reckons there's nothing wrong with you, you've got to train.' But he'd go limping off all the time. Eventually, he went to a specialist in Southampton who did a scan which showed two bones floating about in his ankle. They couldn't even operate because they thought it might cripple him. He came back and played a bit of non-league stuff for Dorchester, but he could barely walk while he was playing, so it wasn't really worth it.

Jamie could have gone to any club in the country when he was 15. In fact, Jamie signed forms for Tottenham, and it was a done deal that when he left school, he'd go and play for them. But about eight months before he left, he changed his mind. He thought he'd get stuck playing youth football at Tottenham for the next few years and wanted to play league football instead. Even though he was only 15, he thought he was good enough to get in the team.

I did everything to try to persuade him to go to Tottenham, told him how great it would be, that he'd be mad to turn down the opportunity to play for such a big club, but he wouldn't have it. I even fell out with Tottenham manager Terry Venables over it. Terry assumed that because I was Bournemouth's manager, I wanted him to play for me and I'd talked Jamie out of going to White Hart Lane. That simply wasn't the case.

Luckily, it worked out perfect for Jamie at Bournemouth, who were in the old Division Two at the time. He'd been training with the first team since he was at school, so everyone already knew him.

His dad being the manager wasn't hard for him because he was a good player and the other lads knew it. If you're no good and your dad's the manager, it must be difficult.

Jamie made his debut at West Ham by accident. Shaun Brooks was taken ill on the coach and a few of the lads, including Paul Miller, who had played for Tottenham for ten years and won a couple of FA Cups, said to me, 'Gaffer, who you gonna play instead?'

'I dunno.'

'You gonna play Jamie?'

'No.'

'Gaffer, if he wasn't your son, you'd play him.'

'I don't know about that.'

'You would. He should play. We want him to play.'

And that was it, Jamie was in the first team at 16.

Jamie was only 17 when I sold him to Liverpool, although he really wasn't keen on going, and I wasn't keen on letting him go.

Bournemouth played at Birmingham and Ron Yeats, Liverpool's chief scout, was watching. Ron went back to Anfield and gave a glowing report about Jamie to Liverpool manager Kenny Dalglish. After that, I had Kenny ringing me up every minute of every day: 'Harry, I've got to have him! Let him come up for a week, just to have a look around.'

I loved Kenny, but I said, 'Ken, it's difficult. He's in my first team, he wants to play league football and he's not going to get in Liverpool's team, because he's still only 17. And he doesn't want to be playing with the other kids.'

But Kenny replied, 'He will be in my team.'

So we went up to Liverpool for four days, Jamie trained with the first-team squad, and I took Kenny's word. Jamie signed for Liverpool and Kenny put him on the bench straightaway.

A few weeks later, Kenny resigned, and Jamie was suddenly out on a limb. It wasn't Kenny's fault, he obviously had very good reasons to step down, but when Graeme Souness replaced him as manager, he didn't know anything about Jamie. Graeme's job was to run the first team, and as far as he was concerned, Jamie was just some 17-year-old kid. For a while, Jamie was playing in the reserves and training with the youth team. But he rung me up one day and said, 'Dad, I'm in the squad to play Auxerre in the UEFA Cup.' And that was that, he never looked back.

Having a son and a nephew playing Premier League football obviously makes a man proud, but it did cause one or two minor difficulties. One Saturday, Jamie played for Liverpool against West Ham when I was the manager and had Frank Lampard Jr in my team. When Jamie caught Frank in a tackle, Frank had to come off for treatment. Les Sealey, my goalkeeping coach, was sat next to me on the bench, and he said to Frank, 'When you go back on, do him good and proper.'

I was thinking, 'Hold on, Les, he's my son!'

*

SANDRA: *Harry was a good dad. He was a lot of fun, but quite strict as well. He expected the boys to be well-behaved and certainly wouldn't take any nonsense from them. He used to take them everywhere with him. From when Mark was about one year old, he'd be on the training ground at Bournemouth. And then we when we moved to America, they'd both be at the training ground every day. They'd even go with Harry to the Kingdome Stadium in Seattle and play on the pitch while the team was training, kicking the ball in the goal at the other end.*

I was incredibly proud when Jamie was picked to play for England. Mark was as well. He was a good brother, there wasn't a hint of jealousy. He was Jamie's biggest fan and used to follow him everywhere. When Jamie was playing for Liverpool, he'd go up there for every home game. Him and Harry's dad. But it was difficult when Jamie had his injuries. When England played Scotland at Euro '96, we got to Wembley late because we got stuck in traffic. We'd just sat down when Jamie went over and got stretchered off with a broken ankle. He ended up with a pin in his ankle and it made him run differently, which affected his knee. In the end, he had nine operations on that knee. He was unlucky with injuries but at least he played for his country, played for Liverpool and Tottenham, so he had a career to be proud of . . .

*

My dad would watch Jamie playing for Liverpool every week, no matter where. Mum and Dad idolised my kids. On the Friday, my mum would make my dad a couple of cheese and mustard pickle rolls and another one to give Jamie after the match. One week, Jamie dropped him at the train station and Steve McManaman was in the car with them. Next time I saw Mum, she said to me, 'Your dad felt terrible, because he had a roll for Jamie and not for his mate Steve.'

'Mum, Steve's probably getting 30 grand a week, I'm sure he can buy himself a cheese and pickle roll if he wants one!'

'Oh, no, you can't give Jamie one and not Steve ... '

Every week after that, Dad would take two rolls, one for Jamie and one for Macca. Mum would put extra butter in Macca's, because she'd seen how skinny his legs were and thought he needed building up.

Bringing up kids isn't easy, that's for sure. But if you teach them to be polite and nice to people, you can't go too far wrong.

14
FURRY FRIENDS

'I couldn't hurt anything, whether it's an elephant or a fly ...'

It's a good job I like animals, because there were enough of them in the jungle with me. I didn't know what half of them were, but that didn't stop me from having a little chat with them from time to time. I love animals almost as much as I love football, whether it's horses, donkeys, fish or birds. In fact, I honestly think that animals deserve the same protection as humans.

I feed the foxes, even though I'm not supposed to. And I also love feeding the squirrels. I'll be in the garden at 5am, even if there's snow on the ground, filling up the bird feeders and tables. When I was still managing, I couldn't leave for work without feeding them first. I'd just hate to think of them going hungry. Some days, I'll see a robin fly past the back window and go out looking for it. I'll throw some bread out and if it comes back, it will make my morning.

I'm passionate about animals being looked after properly and not being harmed. I couldn't hurt anything, whether it's an elephant or a fly. And I certainly wouldn't be happy if anyone ever did anything to one of my dogs. I read all the time about animals being abused and used for illegal sports, and it makes me sick. A few years ago, there was a story in the papers about a donkey that was being made to abseil in Russia. I read about it, got involved and the *Sun* ended up buying the donkey and sending it to a riding school in Moscow. The front-page headline in the *Sun* was: 'Redknapp signs Russian donkey.' I'm told Roman Pavlyuchenko, one of my strikers at Tottenham, was quite worried.

I also read about these trophy hunters, shooting elephants and giraffes and what not, and I just find it unbelievable that anyone would want to do anything like that. What do you gain from shooting something like that? It's bloody disgusting. You've got these beautiful animals wandering about, minding their own business, and some idiot comes along and kills them. I've been on a safari in South Africa and seen the elephants walking about with their little ones, drinking at a waterhole. Look at the size of them, they're as big as buses, and they just stand there looking straight at you. So it's not even as if it's a challenge shooting an elephant. How could anyone miss?

I'll tell you a funny story about that trip to South Africa. Portsmouth had been out in Nigeria, playing a game against Man

Utd. Before coming back, we stopped off in South Africa for a couple of games, and the chairman offered to take us all on a three-day safari. The evening before we were meant to head out, I said to the boys, 'We're off in the morning at six, so you need to be down here at five-thirty. There'll be coffee and muffins, and then we'll jump on some trucks and go out and see the elephants and all the other animals.' I had about ten African players in my team at the time and, that night, about five of them came up to me and said, 'Gaffer, we are from Africa. We have seen elephants and lions all our life. We don't want to get up at five o'clock.' So the following morning, about three of us went on safari and the rest of them stayed in bed.

There weren't many animals roaming the streets of east London, but my uncle had a loft full of pigeons that he used to race. He'd meet his mates down the pub and they'd head off all over the country, as far as Scotland. They'd get up there, let these pigeons go and chase them back down to London. My uncle would get back to his loft, take the ring off his pigeon and leg it to the pub. First one to clock in was the winner and would win a leg of lamb or bag of mince.

It's very important to have passions and, as I've already explained, horses have been a big part of my life since I was very young. I love the Cheltenham Festival, that's some of the best racing there is. But I'd rather sit at home and watch it on television. Good luck to people who want to go to Cheltenham and get boozed up and unwind, but that doesn't appeal to me at all. I don't want to be stood there drinking champagne while everyone's shouting and singing. That's not my scene. Royal

Ascot is even worse. You drive out of there after a day's racing and all you see are people lying about on the roadside drunk, girls who can hardly walk, with their dresses over their heads and even blokes in morning suits having punch-ups. I don't know what makes people want to behave like that, but that's how it is now.

I go to the racing because I love the horses and the sport, not because it's an occasion or an event. It doesn't even have to be horses racing: years ago, I used to watch an old trainer called Louie Dingwall train her horses on the beach near where I lived. I like to go to the little tracks midweek, when it's quiet. I can go on my own quite easily to tracks like Wincanton or Fontwell, and find somewhere quiet at the back of the stand. My perfect scenario is Newbury on a lovely winter's day, all wrapped up warm, sitting there with the *Racing Post* and maybe a bowl of soup. I'll have a chat, study the form, watch the horses in the paddock and then watch them racing. That'll do me.

It's not just the horses I love, I also think the jockeys are incredible people. Talk about bravery, those people are as hard as nails. I'll sometimes watch them on a frosty winter's morning, schooling horses that have never jumped before, riding them into a fence for the first time. They'll approach at speed, and you know that if they hit the fence, both horse and jockey could sustain terrible injuries. It's frightening to watch. When I see a horse fall and the jockey stay down, I worry he or she won't get up. A jockey like Tony McCoy probably broke every bone in his body during his career. He'd sustain an injury that would put a footballer out for months, but Tony would be back riding again a couple of days later.

The dogs were more my thing back when I was younger, and the first time I went to the races was to Fontwell, with the West Ham goalkeeper Jim Standen and our centre-half David Bickles, who were both massive punters. I remember standing out there in the middle of the course and thinking, 'This is special.' And I also vividly remember 100–1 shot Foinavon winning the 1967 Grand National because my mum had him in the sweepstake at her factory. She won about a fiver, which was quite a lot of money in those days We were all listening to the race on the radio, shouting and dancing around the kitchen.

The first horse I owned was Slick Cherry, while I was manager at Bournemouth. 'Slick' because the horse's mother was called Slick Chick, 'Cherry' because Bournemouth are nicknamed the Cherries. A couple of the directors and a few friends were involved and we had a lot of fun with her. She was a flat horse who became a hurdler and was trained by David Elsworth, up at Whitsbury in Hampshire. I used to go up there on a Sunday morning and watch the horses work. David also had the great Desert Orchid in his yard at the time, and we'd watch him on the gallops, which was an awesome sight.

We had some nice wins with Slick Cherry, including a lovely 7–1 touch at Chepstow. One of my horses winning a race doesn't compare to winning a football match and picking up three points, but it's still a great feeling. When I came back from Italy after my car accident in 1990 (I'll tell you more about that later), I was in hospital when Slick Cherry won at Windsor. My friends phoned me from the course, told me about the win and put Frankie Dettori, who'd ridden Slick Cherry to victory, on the phone to say hello. That was a nice little pick-me-up.

Moviesta was probably the best horse I had. He won big races at Goodwood and Doncaster, although I was working when he won the King George Stakes in 2013. I watched it on the TV at the training ground and was jumping around my office like a man possessed. Moviesta should have won the Prix de l'Abbaye at Longchamp, but got beat by a few inches. He kept getting checked and coming again, and a yard past the line he would have been two feet in front. Moviesta died about a year ago. He was just stood in the yard and had a brain haemorrhage.

There's a lot of sadness in racing. I lost two horses in a week at Taunton. One of them was called Bygones In Brid, which we were going to take to Cheltenham. I got there at quarter to two for the two o'clock race, went to the paddock with the jockey and the trainer, and they were telling me what a fantastic hurdler he was. He was a certainty to win that day, a class above the other horses in the race. But when he came to the first hurdle, the sun was so bright in his eyes, he stepped into it, went down and broke his neck.

Within 20 seconds of the race starting, I'd lost my horse. I was in bits, and while I was stood there, this fella came up to me and went, ''Arry, can I have a picture of you with my wife?' So I'm stood there for about three minutes while this bloke is trying to get his camera to work, and eventually he says, 'Give us a smile, 'Arry!' Meanwhile, my horse is lying on the track dead.

Those thoroughbred horses are so powerful but so fragile at the same time. Even if they break a leg they shoot them. Seeing the screen around a fallen horse is one of the saddest sights in racing. It's awful leaving a track without your horse, because you get to love them so much. But that's what they're bred to do.

I currently own ten horses and I've got my own little stable in a village called Piddletrenthide, where a guy called Nick Mitchell does the training. One horse I recently bought that might be decent is Shakem Up'Arry. Watch this space. I might be looking to get out of it, but I enjoy going down there and watching these little kids, young girls and boys, riding these great big National Hunt horses. They have to walk about a mile up the road to get to the gallops, and there will be cars whizzing by. Those horses could bolt and take off at any minute, but they somehow manage to keep control of them.

Even when I've bought race horses that have been no good, I've never taken them to the sales, because those horses get sold as meat. It's horrible at those sales. They'll bring a horse in and someone will shout, '£800? Sold!' And then they'll get taken away, chopped up and eaten. Instead, I find an owner for them. I bought an expensive horse once, which never really amounted to much, and a lady we knew said, 'I've got a friend who wants a horse.'

I said, 'I might have just the thing. It cost me £60,000, it's only four, but it's too slow.'

So I gave her friend this horse, and a short while later she started sending me bills for £900 a month. I phoned her up and said, 'I gave you a lovely horse for nothing, I'm not keeping it in stables for the next 15 years!'

She said, 'But I can't afford to keep her.'

Anyway, I found someone else to look after it, a lady with a nice field. There's no way I would have had it put down, not a chance.

Another thing I like about the horses is that you get to meet a real range of people, and I like talking to them all. Although, sometimes, I don't know who I'm talking to. A few years ago, I was in a casino when this kid introduced himself as the jockey Lee Topliss. He seemed like a nice kid and I befriended him. He'd give me betting tips, and I'd give him tickets to the football. Soon, he was everywhere: at every Tottenham home game, in the directors' box at Man Utd. One day, the football agent Willie McKay phoned and asked me if I still spoke to Lee Topliss. When I said yes, Willie said, 'He's not actually the jockey Lee Topliss. He's a potman at a pub in Newmarket.' This kid had been conning me for three years, and it wasn't just me he'd been scamming.

But you also get to mix with slightly more refined people in racing. One day, Jamie rung me and said, 'What you up to tonight? Fancy coming out for dinner?' I thought he might pay the bill for a change, so I said yes. When I walked in, I sat down opposite this young girl and started chatting away. I had been introduced, but I didn't catch her name.

She says to me, 'Do you like horse racing, Harry?'

'Oh yeah, I love it. My nan was a bookie's runner in the East End. When I was a kid, she used to take all the bets off the old girls on her street.'

This girl starts laughing and says, 'My grandmother loves racing as well.'

'Really?'

'Yes, last year her horse won the Gold Cup at Ascot.'

I thought, 'Blimey, her nan must have a few quid.'

So I asked her the horse's name, she told me and I thought, 'I'm pretty sure the Queen owns that horse . . . '

Suddenly it dawned on me who she was: Princess Beatrice.

Afterwards, Jamie said to me, 'You didn't have a clue who that was, did you?'

He was right, I didn't.

Alex Ferguson loved his racing as well, as did a lot of managers and players. When one of my teams played at Old Trafford, Fergie would call me into his office to watch the 2.45 at Wetherby or wherever. People thought I was in the dressing room, going through tactics with my team on a whiteboard, but me and Alex would be having a bet.

I'd say to him, 'Alex, I should probably get back to my lads.'

'No, you're fine, Harry.'

'It's alright for you, you've got a fantastic team, my lot need a bit of geeing up ... '

But you've got the be careful with the gambling. I've been lucky in that I've managed to control it, it's always been an enjoyable hobby. But gambling, whether it's on the horses or internet casinos, has ruined a lot of footballers' lives. Even today, when top footballers are on tens of thousands of pounds a week, gambling can make them skint. It's just so easy to have a punt nowadays, very different to when my nan used to collect illegal bets on her street. Not only have you got all the racing channels on TV, but there are thousands of websites which will take your money at the click of a button. When you had to pay money over a counter it felt like you were spending real money. You'd give the bookie £50, your horse would finish nowhere and you'd feel a sting. Nowadays, you can burn through thousands of pounds and only notice it when you get sent your bank statement at the end of the month.

I also love my dogs to bits. When me and Sandra first got married, we had a boxer, but he died when he was about ten. We went years without a dog but one year we looked after Jamie's dog when he went on holiday for a week, and we just loved having him around. So one day I brought home a British bulldog. We lost Buster on our wedding anniversary one year. We went out for dinner and when we got home, old Buster had suffered a heart attack. We were devastated. But now we've got two more British bulldogs, Barney and Lulu. They're placid little dopey dogs with no aggression in them whatsoever. In fact, they're such a soft touch, they're always being attacked by other dogs, no matter how big or small they are. I missed them almost as much as Sandra while I was in the jungle.

The most relaxing thing for me is walking them on the beach where I live. Some nights when it's warm they'll go for a paddle. We might walk for a couple of miles, and I can just shut down for an hour or so. I'll also chuck them in the back of my smelly old Ford Focus and take them over the golf course, although I'm not really allowed. I try to go when it's dark and there's no one around, but I was over there the other day and a bloke started shouting at me from about 200 yards away. I called the dogs and started walking the other way, but this bloke started running after me.

When he reached me, he said, 'Oi! This is private property.'

'Sorry mate.'

'Oh, it's Harry isn't it? Sorry, I didn't know it was you, you can do what you want ... '

Another time, it was pitch black and you could barely see, but some bloke was out practising. He comes up to me and says, 'Are you a member here?'

'No.'

'Well I am.'

'Congratulations.'

'Gaffer? Is that you?'

It was Clive Grout, who played for me at Bournemouth. His old man was a bank manager, so I said to him, 'You always were a fuckin' snob, Grouty!'

I'm almost as soppy about my dogs as I am about my grandkids. They deserve my respect just like a human. That's how I treat animals, as my mates.

15
STREET SMARTS

'You've got to be savvy to survive ...'

Nowadays, if a player wants a transfer, he won't talk to managers, he'll talk to his agent, who will then talk to chairmen or chief executives. Managers at the highest level no longer have anything to do with transfer deals. But years ago, if you wanted to buy someone, you'd get on the phone to the player you fancied, bring him in for a chat and have a conversation about how you saw him fitting into the team and how much he might earn. Conversation over, the player would sign a contract and start training with you a few days later. But it was a cut and thrust world. And in a world like that, you get sharp or die.

I left school without a single qualification to my name, but you have to be streetwise to get on in the East End. And in the days before agents and directors of football held sway, a manager required a lot of street smarts and very refined people skills, otherwise they'd never have signed anyone. But I didn't always get my man, because sometimes there were managers wilier than me. Many years ago, I was supposed to sign a lad called Ian Woan, who was playing for non-league Runcorn. Me and my chief scout drove all the way from Bournemouth to watch him play on a freezing cold Tuesday night and we absolutely loved him. The plan was for Ian to come down and sign for Bournemouth the following day. Instead, I got a phone call from his dad, who said he wouldn't be able to make it and could they come down the following day instead. I really wanted to get the deal done, because it had been in the papers that he was set to sign, but his dad wouldn't have it.

Meanwhile, in Nottingham, Brian Clough was in his office looking at Teletext on his telly. He saw this story about Ian Woan signing for Bournemouth and said to his staff, 'Bournemouth seem to do well with non-league players, who's this Woan from Runcorn? Anybody know him?' One of his scouts said, 'I know the manager at Runcorn, I'll give him a ring and see if the deal's been done.' So the Runcorn manager told the Notts Forest scout that Ian wasn't due to sign until tomorrow. Not only that, he said he was miles too good for Bournemouth. When the scout reported this conversation back to Cloughie, Cloughie said, 'How much have Bournemouth offered him?' The scout said, '£40,000.' And Cloughie said, 'Offer him £60,000.'

Later that same night, I got a phone call from Ian's dad: 'Sorry, Harry, we've had Notts Forest on the phone, Ian's going there instead ... '

Then there was the Amdy Faye transfer saga. Amdy was technically an Auxerre player when I included him in my Portsmouth side to play a pre-season friendly against Kilmarnock. He was suspended at the time, and he'd told Auxerre he had the flu so he didn't have to go in for training. His agent got him over to train with us. And when I threw him in against Kilmarnock, he was the best player on the pitch by miles. I wanted to sign him, but we were still trying to agree a fee with Auxerre when other clubs started coming in for him, including Aston Villa and Middlesbrough. His agent had tipped them off and they had scouts there watching him play against Kilmarnock. Suddenly, every club in England was phoning the hotel we were staying in, as well as sending faxes, saying: 'DON'T SIGN FOR PORTSMOUTH.'

So I went to reception and said, 'Look, no telephone calls to Mr Faye's room.' I also destroyed all the faxes – I ripped them up and stuffed them in the bin.

The following day, we were having lunch and the receptionist came over and said, 'Mr Redknapp, do you still want me to stop all calls to Mr Faye's room?' Everyone was looking at me as if to say, 'What's going on?'

Meanwhile, the Auxerre president had made contact with Amdy and was telling him about all these bigger clubs who wanted him. So before I caught a plane back home to Bournemouth, I said to our reserve coach Andy Awford, 'We've put Amdy in a hotel in Portsmouth, keep an eye on him and don't let him escape. He knows other clubs are after him.'

On the Sunday, me and Sandra went to watch Jamie playing for Tottenham. We'd left the ground and were on our way to Jamie's for a barbecue when Andy Awford rung me and said, 'Harry, I've just been to the hotel. Amdy's gone.'

'What do you mean, he's gone? I told you not to let him out of your sight!'

'He's disappeared. I think he must be on his way back to France.'

I said to Sandra, 'Forget the barbecue, we're going to Heathrow Airport to capture Amdy Faye.'

I got to Heathrow, found out which terminal flights to Paris were going from and started looking for him. And by an absolute miracle, I found him. I said, 'Amdy, Amdy, where you going?'

'I go home. I go home.'

'No, Amdy, you can't go home, you have to come with me.'

'Where, coach? Why, coach?'

So I bundled him into the car and took him down to Poole with me and Sandra. When we got in the house, he took one look at the dogs and said, 'Oh no, bulldogs!'

'Amdy, if you try to escape, those bulldogs will bite your bollocks off.'

'Oh no, bulldogs!'

He wouldn't stop going on about my bulldogs, so I locked him in a room upstairs. The next morning, I knocked on his door and he didn't answer. I said to Sandra, 'I think he might have done another runner.' But I got him up eventually, and Sandra made him breakfast before I whisked him to Portsmouth's ground. He agreed a fee, passed his medical and we got him signed.

I still got done by the FA. They had me up for playing someone who belonged to another club, under the name 'Henry', as in the France and Arsenal legend Thierry. I had to sit before a committee, and they said to me, 'You played this player who belonged to Auxerre and put him down under a wrong name.'

'Well, first of all, I didn't know he was under contract with another club. And when I asked him what his name was, he kept saying "Henry". I thought that was his name, but he was trying to tell me he knew Thierry Henry. And if you believe that, you'll believe anything.'

They started laughing and said, 'Harry, just piss off.'

That was the end of that one, and Amdy was a great player for me at Portsmouth.

John 'Willo' Williams, who I bought for Bournemouth in 1986, might have been the best signing I ever made. I was in the car park when Willo pulled in, and he had a girl in the passenger seat. I said a cheery hello and invited them both inside, but the girl didn't move. So John said to me, 'She's alright, Harry, she'll stay in the car.'

'Nah, come inside, we won't be long.'

'No, honestly, she'll stay in the car.'

'Don't be daft, come in and have a cup of tea … '

So we got in the office, and as I was going through the contract details with Willo, I said to this girl, 'What do you do?'

'I'm a nurse.'

'Oh, wonderful, there's a hospital just down the road, we'll get you a job there.'

This went on for a couple of hours, before the three of us went for a nice walk on the beach. The following week, Willo moved down to Bournemouth and I asked him whether he wanted us to look into getting a job for his girlfriend. It was only then that Willo told me he'd only met her a few days earlier, in a nightclub in Stoke. He'd spent the night with her, brought her straight down to Bournemouth for a short break and never seen her again. At least she got a cup of tea and a couple of custard creams out of it.

Also when I was manager at Bournemouth, Maidstone United had a lad called Mark Newson who I'd been after for some time. I found out he was going for a trial at Tottenham, before someone phoned to tell me Mark wasn't signed to a contract at Maidstone because he was claiming dole money. So I called Mark, got him down to Bournemouth and wouldn't let him leave until he signed. As soon as the deal was done, I rung Maidstone manager Barry Fry.

'Hello Barry, Harry Redknapp. I'm just phoning to let you know I've signed Mark Newson.'

'Have you been drinking? He's going to Spurs for £200,000.'

'Sorry, Barry. I've signed him.'

'What do you mean, you've signed him? We haven't agreed a fee!'

'There is no fee. He's not registered with Maidstone.'

Barry exploded, started ranting and raving about sending a couple of heavies round to shoot my kneecaps off. I said goodbye and put the phone down. The next day, Maidstone's chairman phoned me. He started off by being very apologetic about Barry's behaviour, before trying to gently persuade me that the gentlemanly thing would be for Bournemouth to pay them some money. But when I wouldn't budge, he started threatening me as well. The day after that, I got another call from Barry, who hadn't calmed down at all.

'I'm sending two fuckin' geezers down to see you! You're fuckin' dead! I'm warning you, Redknapp, you won't have any kneecaps left!'

I just started laughing and put the phone down again. The following day, me and Bournemouth's managing director Brian Tiler were in the office when we saw a car pull up outside and Barry, his chairman and some other bloke we didn't recognise jumped out. Me and Brian legged it out the back, across the pitch and over the turnstiles, before jumping into a waiting car. Mark was brilliant for Bournemouth. He captained the side when we won the Third Division title and we sold him to Fulham for £100,000 a couple of years later.

But for all the competitiveness, there was also great civility and respect between managers. I always enjoyed having a glass of wine with Alex Ferguson after a game. I say 'enjoy', but usually it was excruciating. My teams didn't win very often at Old Trafford, so I'd usually have the hump. And on the odd occasion we did win, Alex would have the hump, because he wasn't a good loser either. But we'd still have a drink, it was just something you had to do.

There were a few players I'm glad I missed out on. When I was managing West Ham, someone said to me one day, 'Gaffer, George Weah's on the phone.' George Weah was at AC Milan at the time and had recently been voted the best player in the world, so I obviously thought it was a wind-up.

Anyway, I got on the phone and said, 'How you going, George?'

'Yes, I'm good.'

'Looking good for your team this year … '

I was just humouring him, but he started talking about all the players he was going to be playing with that year – Roberto Baggio, Zvonimir Boban, Dejan Savićević – and suddenly I thought, 'Bloody 'ell, it is 'im!'

'I've seen your team play, Harry. They're good, but you don't score enough goals. My cousin is a fantastic player, you should take a look at him.'

I didn't hear anything more from George, but after he got off the phone to me, he rang Graeme Souness, who was manager at Southampton. Graeme signed George's cousin on a one-match contract and brought him on against Leeds. He replaced the injured Matt Le Tissier, one of the most talented players this country has ever produced, and lasted 50 minutes before being substituted himself. It transpired that the bloke I spoke to who knew so much about AC Milan was actually a mate of this kid's from university.

There were also players I desperately wanted to sign who were blind to my charms. When I was at Tottenham, I thought I had Eden Hazard in the bag, especially after I spent two hours with him in a hotel room in Paris. In hindsight, maybe that's why he signed for Chelsea instead. And then there were the players I was desperate to get rid of. At Portsmouth, I had a centre-forward called Benjani Mwaruwari, who we'd bought from France. He didn't score in his first 14 games, and when he used to do shooting practice, I'd have to ring Southampton Airport to make sure there were no planes taking off. But the crowd loved him and I loved him, because he never stopped working. Benji did score the goal against Wigan that kept us up, and the following season he started to bang a few goals in. So suddenly, I had Man City manager Sven-Göran Eriksson on the phone, offering us £9 million for Benji. Only Sven would have offered that much.

I went straight to Benji and said, 'Benji, you've got to go, Man City want you.'

'But I like it here, boss. I won't go.'

'No, Benji, I don't think you understand. Man City are a big club, you'll love it up there, you've got to go!'

In the end, I was shoving him out of the door. After getting him to Southampton Airport, I rung him a couple of times to see how he was getting on. He let one flight go, he let another flight go, and eventually someone had to drag him onto the runway and push him through the door of the plane. It was transfer deadline day, but he only arrived in Manchester at 10.30 in the evening, an hour and a half before the transfer window closed. They rushed him to Man City's stadium and got cracking on the paperwork. I was sat in my office staring at the fax machine with my fingers crossed, and confirmation of the deal came through about a minute before midnight. Good old Benji, and good old Sven.

Football changed a lot between me managing Bournemouth and selling Benji to Man City for £9 million, but you needed the same skills. In any rough and tumble and often ruthless environment, you've got to be savvy to survive.

16
A LITTLE BIT OF POLITICS

'What do politicians know about real life?'

Injustice makes me angry. People see me living in a nice house and driving a nice car and think, 'Oh, what would he know about injustice?' But I didn't exactly grow up rich. And it's sad to see people who are struggling to eat or are homeless, especially when the weather gets cold or it's raining. I don't know what the answer is, but I try to help in any small way I can. And I think that anybody with the money and the time should do the same.

Sandra will do some cooking and I'll take it down to the shelter. I love doing it, but it makes me sad. It's difficult, because you don't know what problems homeless people have had to make them end up like that. And some people don't want to be helped. There's a homeless boy I speak to most days, as well as giving him a cup of tea and a few quid. He's a Geordie boy and a lovely fella. The other week, he had a couple of black eyes and a broken nose. Apparently, a couple of blokes had weed on him, and when he got up, they kicked and punched him in the face. I had the idea of getting him cleaned up and making him my driver. But when I spoke to him about it, he didn't seem interested. He's obviously got his reasons, and you just don't know these people's stories. But I'd like it if this kid could somehow get out of the terrible situation he's in.

I'm not big into politics. I haven't got a clue what's going on with Brexit. I've reached the stage of thinking, 'What's gonna happen is gonna happen.' But whatever happens, it's not going to kill us. We've just got to get on with it. I just don't understand why the political parties can never agree on anything. It never seems to happen that Theresa May comes up with an idea and Jeremy Corbyn says, 'Hey, great idea, Theresa. Love it. It will be good for the country, it's going to help everybody, let's do it.' Instead, one side will say something and the other side will say, 'Nah, that's a load of rubbish.'

What do politicians know about real people and real life anyway? They're in another world, were brought up differently, went to different schools. How can they possibly understand people who live on council estates in the East End? When was the last time they went there? Probably never in some cases. That's why when I was growing up in the East End, everybody was staunch Labour. Nobody ever thought of voting Conservative. But nowadays, none of the parties seem to have much connection with the man and woman on the street.

If I had a magic wand, I'd put the pensions up, make sure everyone had a decent place to live, give more money to the NHS and give nurses a big raise. The facilities in some hospitals are terrible and the poor staff are overworked and horribly underpaid. It's madness when you think that a footballer can earn 300 grand a week and a nurse might only be on 20-odd grand a year.

Racism upsets me. I can't believe it still goes on in football grounds. I played with John Charles, who was the first black man to play for West Ham, and Clyde Best, who came over from Bermuda and was a big pal of mine. Clyde wrote a letter to West Ham and arrived in England when he was only 17. He'd paid his own fare, travelled on his own and when he turned up at Upton Park, the gate was locked. He was stopping people in the street and asking them, 'Excuse me, do you know where the West Ham footballers stay?' He must have thought we all stayed in digs together, he didn't have a clue.

Clyde went and lived with Clive Charles, another black player at West Ham, and they still had an outside toilet with newspaper instead of toilet roll. Clyde put up with some horrendous abuse. People threw bananas at him on the pitch, he received a letter from someone threatening to throw acid in his face. But Clyde stood up to everything that was chucked his way, it all just seemed to bounce off him.

Clyde was the loveliest boy you'd ever wish to meet and very laid-back. When he was managing Bermuda, me and Frank Lampard Sr went over there for a bit of a holiday and to do a bit of coaching with the kids. But when the kids turned up to training, Clyde wasn't there. He'd got his dates muddled up. That was typical Clyde, everything could always wait until tomorrow.

I was sitting there the other day and I had a great idea about making a documentary about Clyde. I could interview him, take him back to Upton Park and to Mrs Charles's house, if it's still there. Because Clyde and those boys were pioneers. When I was growing up, the East End was famous for its Jewish boxers. Lots of great Jewish champions came out of the East End, because they grew up hard. Now we've got so many fantastic black and mixed-race kids coming through. Like Jewish kids in my day, they're often from poor backgrounds and are very hungry. They're becoming the lifeblood of our game.

There were hardly any women involved in football when I was still playing. The only women you saw around a club made the tea or did the laundry, and there were hardly any in the stands. Sandra didn't even watch me play. But I've also seen attitudes towards women change for the better down the years, and women themselves have changed a lot since I was a kid.

It was a man's world back then, but not anymore. There's nothing wrong with a woman wanting to stay at home and look after the house and the kids, but women are much more go-getting now, have their own ambitions and careers. And the girls are very different. They stand up for themselves a lot more than they used to, are a lot more confident and can take better care of themselves. Now, you've got women playing a good standard of football and who are very knowledgeable pundits who understand the game. And as long as they know what they're talking about, I've got no problem with it.

The world would be a better place if everybody was just nice and helped each other out. If all political parties had that as a philosophy, we'd be in a far better place.

17
CHEATING DEATH

'You only get one life ... '

When I hit 70, I started to worry. I'd be sitting there thinking, 'Fuckin' 'ell, time's going too quick.' That's what happens when you get old, time starts speeding up. Where have the last ten years gone? And will the next ten years go even quicker? That's why it was so terrifying when they put me in that coffin in the jungle. When they put the lid on, I thought, 'This feels a bit too real.' But the passing of time and the realisation that you're not here forever also makes you think that you've got to make the most of every day that comes along.

Only recently, Gordon Banks died, which means four of that World Cup-winning team of 1966 have gone: Banksy,

Bobby Moore, Ray Wilson and Alan Ball. And when people you remember as vibrant young men start dying, it gets you thinking about your own mortality. I was also standing right next to Glenn Hoddle when he had a cardiac arrest. I'd been with Glenn all morning in the BT studios and he looked fantastic. It was his birthday, we were all having a laugh and a joke and suddenly, crash, he was on the floor. I knew right away that something was terribly wrong. Luckily, a guy from the sound department knew first aid and saved Glenn's life. The whole time this fella was working on him, I was thinking, 'Please God, let him be okay.' You couldn't meet a nicer bloke than Glenn, he's a lovely person, so that was a very traumatic day.

I let the fitness slip a bit after I came out of the jungle because I was too busy with other stuff. But I usually like to do two or three days a week in the gym, an hour in the morning. I absolutely love it, it sets me up for the day. Not that I really needed to look after my weight after the jungle, because I lost about 18lb while I was in there. And I was only about 12st to begin with. When I first met Sandra, I was 10st 6lb, so I'm around about my fighting weight.

All in all I'm in pretty good nick, though my knee sometimes gives me some gip. Not long ago, I went to my physio in London. I checked in, sat down, picked up the *Evening Standard* and there were a couple of lads stretching, both wearing baseball caps. All of a sudden, one of them said, 'Hi Harry!' I looked up and said, 'Alright mate,' and gave him a thumbs-up. I looked at him again and thought, 'I know that geezer from somewhere. Did he play for me?' Then I thought I tumbled who it was. I went up to the girl on reception and said, 'Excuse me. Is that Prince Harry?' She confirmed it was. So I went up to him and said, 'How you doing, Harry?' and we ended up having a nice chat.

The first time I was properly worried about my health was a few years ago, when I had a tumour removed from my bladder. I knew something wasn't right, but it was Sandra who persuaded me to go to the doctor. Fortunately, the tumour wasn't malignant and I was up and about after a couple of days. There was also the time I was on the running machine and I felt pains in my chest and was struggling for breath. I went to see the doctor, he referred me to a specialist and a couple of days later I was in hospital. I'd had narrow or blocked arteries for some time and had been taking tablets for it, but they just needed a bit of a clean-up.

I also had a heart scare during my trial for tax evasion. The case had been dragging on for years, I was still managing Tottenham and it was a very stressful time. One morning, me and Jamie went for a round of golf, but as I was walking down the first hole, I couldn't breathe. Jamie said I'd gone grey. Jamie tried to get me to go to the doctor, but I said I'd wait and see. The following morning, I got on the running machine and had to stop after a couple of minutes. I knew something wasn't right with me, so I saw the club doctor and he took me straight to hospital. That night, I had what they call a coronary angioplasty, and after that I was right as rain. There's no point worrying about these things, what will be will be.

It's been tough for Sandra, seeing me go through the mill. After leaving Portsmouth, she got me to sit down in the living room and gave me a box. I thought, 'Oh, that's nice, she's bought me a present. Maybe it's a nice bottle of wine or something.' But when I opened it, it was a kit to take your blood pressure with! Luckily, at least the old blood pressure was okay.

Of course, I've had one very close brush with death. Me and a few other lads went on holiday to Italy for the 1990 World Cup and we were involved in a car crash that killed my good friend Brian Tiler and three Italians. We'd been to see Ireland play Italy in Rome and were on our way home when this other car drove straight through us on the wrong side of the road. I don't remember anything about the impact, because I was asleep at the time, but I suffered a fractured skull, a broken right leg and a nasty gash to my left. When I arrived at the hospital, they thought I was dead. By rights, I should have been.

I was in hospital for 11 days before returning home. It took me quite a while to fully recover and I never regained my sense of smell, which is actually quite handy for somebody who spends a lot of time in dressing rooms. People say that something like that changes you, and for a while I thought that football wouldn't bother me anymore, that it couldn't possibly be the be-all and end-all. But the crash didn't change my sense of perspective for long.

The doctors told me to steer clear of football for at least six months after the crash, and a lawyer told me that if I stayed off work for eight months and said the crash had ruined my career, I'd get a massive settlement and be a rich man. But I was back at Bournemouth only ten weeks later, hiding at the back of the stand in a woolly hat and duffle coat, watching the team play Reading. Not working would have driven me mad. And after that first match back, I gave the goalkeeper, who let in a couple of silly goals, a real bollocking. He looked up at me and said, 'Glad to see you're feeling better, Harry ... '

Despite everything that had happened, football was still as important to me as it had ever been. But that wasn't necessarily a bad thing: if something gives your life purpose, however trivial it might seem to others, that's better than not being interested in anything. You only get one life, so best to give it your best shot.

18
LARGER THAN LIFE

'I managed a lot of idiots ...'

There definitely aren't the characters around now that there were when I was playing. Back then, sportspeople were allowed to express themselves more. Perhaps when there's more at stake, personalities necessarily get toned down.

Muhammad Ali is my all-time favourite sportsman. I remember watching him fight Henry Cooper at Wembley, when Henry knocked him over with that big left hook. Ali looked like he was gone, but he recovered and stopped Henry in the next round, which was what made him so amazing. And if he wasn't a boxer, Ali could have been the greatest defence barrister in the world. I reckon he could have got anyone off any charge.

Football had even more characters than boxing, there were so many big personalities in dressing rooms. When I first joined West Ham, the players ran the club, not the manager. And Malcolm Allison, who was a player just coming to the end of his career, was the guvnor at Upton Park. Nowadays, the players don't even talk to each other on the coach. They're all listening to music and playing computer games. And finding a captain seems to be getting more and more difficult. In fact, I think we've seen the end of those old-school captains, who bossed his team-mates and led by example. John Terry at Chelsea was probably the last of that breed. He was a great, great leader.

We certainly had a lot more fun as players, drinking together in the Black Lion and on the train home from games. But the modern footballer can't really be the same sort of personality as we had in my day. And, to be honest, I've got no time for any player who can't look after himself nowadays, given the rewards they get. Someone like Harry Kane conducts himself right. He's a great professional, no trouble for his manager at all, as he should be. He's on hundreds of thousands of pounds a week, so it would be criminal if he was out getting drunk and behaving like an idiot. And, believe you me, I managed an awful lot of players who behaved like idiots.

When I was manager at West Ham, the players wanted a Christmas party one year. We were nearly bottom of the League, and they'd hired an open-top bus with a jazz band to take them from the training ground in Essex to the West End. I said to Dale Gordon, also known as 'Disco Dale': 'Are you fuckin' mad? You're gonna be riding along on an open-top bus like you've just won the FA Cup, past people digging roads and cleaning offices, for a fraction of what you're earning. These are people who pay to watch you play and pay your wages. And you want to go on an open-top bus drinking and dancing. They'd be well within their rights to throw bricks at you. Never mind an open-top bus, you should be fuckin' hiding. No fuckin' chance it's happening.'

You couldn't make it up. I put the kibosh on it, only for Dale to hire a minibus instead. A Dutch lad called Jeroen Boere set fire to the seats.

When we went out on a Saturday night, we wouldn't feel the need to get fall-over drunk to have a good time. We behaved ourselves. Even today, I don't mind people enjoying themselves on a night out but getting hammered and falling over is not my scene. People probably saw that clip of me singing 'My Way' on New Year's Eve and assumed I was drunk, but I'd probably only had two glasses of wine. In contrast, the West Ham side I managed in the mid-1990s were a bunch of hooligans. After a testimonial game in Bournemouth, the players destroyed a snooker table. After a golf trip, there was a minor riot in the bar. That was particularly mortifying, because I was a member. On another golf trip, Dale Gordon tipped over a buggy and bust his leg. He was never the same player. And let's not forget, these are the things I knew about. What those boys got up to when I wasn't looking doesn't even bear thinking about.

Those lads were a hard group of players to manage. There were some proper lads in that team, people like Julian Dicks, John Moncur and John Hartson. Dicks was hard work. He used to turn up to training on a Harley-Davidson, even though I'm pretty sure he didn't have a licence. When the other lads were warming up, he'd be sitting in the bath eating a packet of crisps and drinking a can of Coke. When the other lads were stretching he wouldn't stretch, he'd be hiding round the back or booting balls into people's gardens. He hated training, and when Julian didn't fancy training, none of them did. When he did want to train, he'd go hell for leather, which would make him dangerous. My first season as Billy Bonds's assistant, our big summer signing was a boy called Simon Webster from Charlton, but he only lasted a few weeks of pre-season before Julian broke his leg. If they were playing a practice match and Billy gave a corner, Julian would start arguing it was a goal-kick. He was like an unruly teenager. And because he was such a strong character and everyone respected him, all the others would follow his lead and be a pain in the arse as well.

But what a player Julian Dicks was. He was hard as nails and had a left foot like a magic wand. He could land a ball on a sixpence from 40 yards away. He was up there with the best left-backs in the world for a while and should have played dozens of times for England. And because that's all the fans saw of Julian, they absolutely adored him. He'd get sent off for a terrible tackle and the fans would start singing his name. We sold him to Liverpool and when I re-signed him, he was a different boy. He'd injured his knee, and when he first came back, he trained with a brace on his leg. And he trained like a demon. He was a much better person second time around, a lot more humble.

Also while I was at West Ham, I saw Paolo Di Canio try to pour a giant barrel of Gatorade over Shaka Hislop's head during a half-time team talk. I was wearing a brand-new suit, so dived under a table. Paolo missed Shaka but got Gatorade all over his lovely white linen suit instead. And there was a lot of collateral damage. At Tottenham, I had a bucket of water dumped over my head by David Bentley, after we'd just qualified for the Champions League and while I was being interviewed on the television. I had to laugh it off, but I was furious because it was disrespectful. If David had ever played for Manchester United, I doubt whether he would have dumped a bucket of water over Sir Alex Ferguson. Alex probably would have sacked him on the spot, live on air. I must admit, I didn't find that funny, even though we'd just beaten Man City to qualify for the Champions League. No, I really wasn't best pleased, but we cleaned my suit up and sold it for charity, so something good came out of it.

I also had Neil 'Razor' Ruddock at West Ham, and he's a larger than life character in every sense, especially if you see him now. He went missing for a couple of weeks when he was supposed to be coming in for treatment on an injury, and when he finally got it contact, he told us he'd had the flu. But a couple of days later, the *News of the World* came out, and they had a cartoon strip of Razor having a fight with his old team-mate Mike Newell at Gleneagles golf course. Apparently, their wives had had a row, the pair of them had jumped in and ended up punching each other and falling over tables.

I fined Razor two weeks' wages, which I thought he'd take on the chin. Instead, he decided to appeal. Before going before an FA board, I spoke to Dave Richards, the FA's chairman, and he told me that Razor had no chance of winning but that we'd still have to schlep up there. We turned up and Razor had this South African barrister with him, who could have been a film star. He was the cleverest man I've ever met in my life. This guy tied me and Dave up in knots. It was embarrassing, a complete mismatch.

After they'd heard all the evidence, Dave and another couple of FA people left the room to deliberate. When they came back in, Dave looked at me and said, 'I'm sorry, Harry, but we'll have to find Mr Ruddock not guilty and overturn his fine.'

Razor looked at me and said, 'Unlucky, 'Arry.'

I couldn't do anything but shrug my shoulders.

Suddenly, the barrister throws some paperwork across the table and says, 'This is my bill. And I don't come cheap.' It was for 30 grand.

Dave said, 'Sorry, this is not a court of law, we don't pay fees; the client will have to pay that.'

I looked over at Razor and said, 'Unlucky, son.' We laugh about it when we see each other now. That was just football.

Football people certainly used to be a lot quirkier, and nobody was quirkier than Brian Clough. When Cloughie wanted to sign Larry Lloyd for Notts Forest, he asked Larry if he had a washing machine. Larry said he had, but that it had broken down. The following morning, there was a knock on Larry's door and when he answered it, there were two blokes standing there with a washing machine. When Larry went in for his first day of training, a couple of old girls said to him, 'Are you Larry Lloyd?' Larry looked all proud and said yes, he was indeed Larry Lloyd. And the old girls said in unison, 'Thanks very much!' It turned out Cloughie had nicked the washing machine from the ground, and the two old girls couldn't do the laundry.

One of my biggest decisions most days is whether to have a sausage or bacon sandwich in the café down the road.

On walk near my house with my dogs – I missed them almost as much as Sandra while I was in the jungle.

I'm a bit of an old softy really. If there's something I can do to help someone, I'll do it.

When Jamie isn't pretending to shower me in a bath for charity, I'm tremendously proud of what he's achieved as a footballer.

Sandra hates being in the limelight more than I do. But sometimes, with a husband as dashing as me, she doesn't have a choice.

I've come a long way since the Burdett Estate in Poplar – here's Sandra translating a conversation between me and Prince Charles.

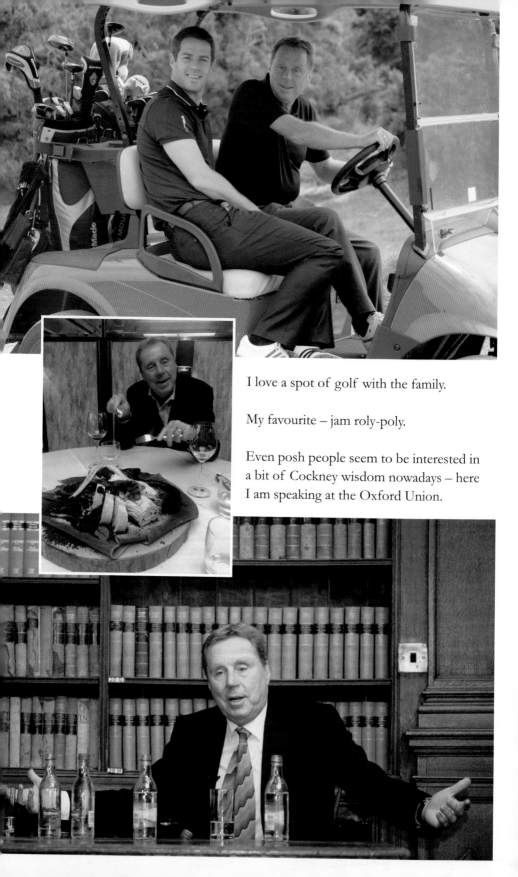

I love a spot of golf with the family.

My favourite – jam roly-poly.

Even posh people seem to be interested in a bit of Cockney wisdom nowadays – here I am speaking at the Oxford Union.

When they put the lid on that coffin I thought, 'This is a bit too real'.

The look on my face says: 'This is not how I expected life to pan out'.

Me and jungle campmate Emily, awaiting the dropping of rats – not a sentence I thought I'd ever say.

Sandra turning up in the jungle was just wonderful. I missed her so much, and I sometimes wonder if I love her too much.

King of the jungle! Who would have thought a bloke in his 70s could have pulled it off?

The jungle crew and friends – I had my doubts, but I'm so glad I went in.

Harry's Heroes – former England stars attempting to get fit. Except for Razor Ruddock.

When Wimbledon's famous 'Crazy Gang' team of the late 1980s played at Forest's City Ground, they brought their stereo with them and turned it up so loud the whole place was shaking. Cloughie sent one of his coaches to Wimbledon's dressing room to tell them to turn their music down. Vinnie Jones answered the door in his pants, turned the music down, but a few minutes later it was louder than ever. This happened a couple more times, before Cloughie finally lost his rag. He marched into the Wimbledon dressing room without knocking, walked straight over to the stereo, picked it up and dropped it on the floor, before walking out again without a word.

Stuart Pearce, who played for Cloughie at Forest, used to tell me all these stories when he came to play for me at West Ham. Apparently, the players wouldn't see Cloughie all week, and then he'd come in on Friday morning and walk his dog around the training ground. One day, the lads were playing five-a-sides and Cloughie shouted over to his full-back Brian Laws, 'You're wasting your time, take my dog for a walk instead.' And Brian did.

The only dealings I had with Cloughie were when I was at Bournemouth and he rang to ask about a player I had called Shaun Teale. I'd bought Shaun from Weymouth for about £40,000 about six months earlier, so when Cloughie asked how much I wanted for him, I said, '£500,000.'

'I'll not give you that, I'll give you £499,999.'

'We'll not fall out over a penny, Brian.'

'Tell the boy he's coming to play for Brian Clough at Nottingham Forest.'

I put the phone down, told the lad he was going to play for Forest in the First Division and didn't hear anything for the rest of the day. Eventually, I phoned Forest and Cloughie's secretary told me he'd gone on holiday to Majorca for ten days and wasn't contactable. I never spoke to Cloughie again, and Shaun Teale never went to Forest.

When my mate Kevin Bond was at Man City, he thought he'd been signed by Cloughie. Kevin's manager at Man City said to him, 'Everything's been agreed, you've just got to go down to Nottingham in the morning and dot the Is and cross the Ts.' When Kevin arrived at Forest, Cloughie's secretary told him to sit outside his office. Ten minutes passed, half an hour passed, and Kevin was still sat there. After about an hour, Cloughie finally emerged, looked at Kevin and said, 'The first thing you want to do, young man, is get your bloody hair cut,' before walking off. Eventually, after another two hours of sitting outside Cloughie's office, Kevin left and drove back to Manchester. That was the end of that: he never heard from Cloughie again.

Steve Claridge, who I signed for Bournemouth, was one of the quirkiest people you could imagine. He'd wear boots of different sizes, because he thought they were lucky. On the way to his first match against York City, he ate six packets of glucose tablets and two Mars Bars on the coach and was sick. During the warm-up, he couldn't walk, and it transpired that he was wearing size six-and-a-half boots, and he was a size eight. Apparently, the bloke in the shop had told him they'd stretch with time. Within two minutes of the game starting, Steve hobbled towards the touchline in pain and said, 'Has anyone got any eights? These boots are killing me.'

When Steve got anxious, he'd shave his hair, a bit at a time. He'd turn up to training and one side of his head would have hair, the other would be bald. But, to be fair to Steve, he was the ultimate professional who played for half the teams in English football.

One night before a big game against Carlisle United, my Bournemouth side stayed in Blackpool, and I told the lads that they weren't allowed to go out. This was back in the days when you had to tell lads not to go out the night before a game, otherwise they would. Blackpool's manager Sam Ellis came to the hotel for a cup of tea and a chat, and I thought all the players were tucked up in bed by ten o'clock. But when I got in the lift, I kept getting lost. I ended up in the basement, then up again, then down again. I got out in the underground car park, wandered around for a bit, and when I opened the lift doors again, six of my players were standing there. The smell of aftershave almost knocked me over, and my captain John Williams was standing there in this white suit, looking like John Travolta.

'What do you think this is,' I said, '*Saturday Night Fever?*'

The evening before Bournemouth beat Manchester United at home in the third round of the FA Cup in 1984, we all went for a promenade on the seafront before going out for a meal at an Italian restaurant. The manager said to our goalkeeper, Ian Leigh, 'If you can keep a clean sheet tomorrow, we'll give you free pizza for life.' Ian was already carrying too much timber, and he wasn't the tallest, so the last thing he needed to be doing was eating pizza every day. But after we won 2–0, Ian was eating pizza for breakfast, lunch and dinner for the next few months. He was quickly turning into the Michelin Man, until I bought the restaurant and told him free pizza was now off the menu.

After that game, the lads went out on the town to celebrate. We were in Division Three and had just knocked the holders out of the FA Cup, so I had no problem with the lads having a few drinks. But just because they'd just pulled off one of the greatest upsets in FA Cup history didn't mean everyone in Bournemouth knew who they were. When they turned up at one nightclub and proudly announced that they were the Bournemouth team who had just knocked Manchester United out of the FA Cup, one of the bouncers said, 'Behave yourselves, the Bournemouth team are already inside.' Another group of lads were masquerading as them, so my lads had to queue up elsewhere.

On John Williams's birthday, his team-mates decided to strip him and leave him on Bournemouth Pier. In fairness to the lads, that took some doing, because Willo was 6ft 2in and strong as an ox. And they were kind enough to let him keep his trainers. Willo lived in Boscombe, which is about two miles down the coast from Bournemouth. No taxi driver in his right mind was going to take him home, and I'm assuming he had no money anyway, unless he had a few notes stashed between his arse cheeks. So Willo had to walk all the way home, sprinting between lampposts and hiding behind trees. The day after Willo got stripped, the boys were like kids on Christmas morning, they could not wait to get into the dressing room and tell me what had happened.

Alan Groves, who I played with at Bournemouth, was one of the biggest personalities I met in football. He was a lorry driver, smoked about 80 fags a day and came into the game late, but he was an incredible footballer and could run like you'd never seen. I played against him when I was at West Ham and he was at Shrewsbury, and we couldn't get near him. It was like a Benny Hill sketch, with about eight of us chasing him all over the pitch. Something was always happening when he was around. Before one game, away at Chesterfield, we got off the coach and a girl dumped a baby into his arms before marching off. It was his, from when he was playing for Shrewsbury. Alan was standing there in the dressing room, holding this baby, before he gave it to a couple of old girls to look after during the game. Sadly, Alan's story doesn't have a happy ending, as he died of a heart attack when he was just 29.

Then there was Robert Prosinečki, who played for me at Portsmouth. Robert had played for Real Madrid and Barcelona, won the European Cup with Red Star Belgrade and finished third at a World Cup with Croatia. But he didn't stop smoking. He'd smoke before the game, at half-time, after the final whistle. He'd have smoked on the pitch if he'd been allowed.

Jimmy Greaves was one of the greatest players I ever saw, but he'd turn up 15 minutes before kick-off, go in the toilet in his suit, have a fag, come out, change into his kit, shake his legs about a bit, then go out and score a hat-trick. I wouldn't recommend the smoking or the drinking, but there's a lot the modern footballer could learn from Jim, who never took football too seriously.

19
MONEY ISN'T EVERYTHING

'I didn't have two farthings to
rub together ... '

I don't know why people seem to be less happy nowadays. But if I had to guess, I'd say it's because life is more complicated. Because I've come from nothing, I'm in a position to say that money doesn't bring you happiness. Don't get me wrong, money can buy you nice luxuries and great experiences. But some of the best times I had in football – and in life – were when I didn't have two farthings to rub together.

Going abroad on holiday didn't enter your mind when I was a kid, it just wasn't an option. I remember going to America for the first time with West Ham and it was like going to Mars. No one went to America back then, but that wasn't really a holiday, that was work. My mum never went abroad – the farthest she ever went was Bournemouth. And the only time my dad went abroad was during the war, and he spent most of that time in a German prison. My first holiday abroad would have been after I married Sandra and we had kids. But we certainly never went abroad while we were courting.

One summer, six of us went on holiday down to Boscombe. It was me, Sandra, Frank Sr, Pat, our West Ham team-mate Roger Cross and his wife Joy. Joy was Pat's best pal from school, and Joy ended up meeting Roger completely independently of Pat, which was another amazing coincidence.

Me and Sandra didn't think we could afford this holiday but changed our minds at the last minute. But because we turned up late, we couldn't get into this grotty little guesthouse that the other four were staying in, so we booked into another place. We turned up at the address, drove down some back street and the owner was out the back of his house. As I walked up to him to tell him we had a booking, I trod straight into some cement he'd spent all day laying. I think that might be the first time Sandra ever called me Mr Pastry. After that, he led us to our quarters. I say quarters, but it was actually two garden sheds. God's honest truth, it was two garden sheds! At least they were next door to each other. They were both full up with tools, and Sandra's had the added bonus of a lawnmower hanging on the wall. Whether our sleeping arrangements had anything to do with the great big footprint I'd put in his doorstep, I never knew, but at least I didn't feel so bad about it.

We stayed there one night and the following morning went back to where the other four were staying. The owner said she didn't have any more room, but that she could squeeze another bed in. So the three boys stayed in one room upstairs, and the girls stayed in another room downstairs.

It was May, so the kids weren't off school and there was hardly anyone around. And we had six days of wall-to-wall sunshine, so we spent all day, every day on the beach. For lunch, we'd buy two chickens from the Woolworths rotisserie, a bit of salad for the girls and eat it off a beach towel. And every night we'd go to the Grill and Griddle and have spaghetti bolognese and ice cream, which cost us about three and sixpence each. Spaghetti bolognese was a bit exotic in those days, although I think we shared a plate of chips with it. And you know what? That was one of the best holidays we ever had – maybe the best – we had an absolute ball, the time of our life. Which just goes to show, lying on a beach in the Maldives makes you no happier than eating chicken off a beach towel in Boscombe. Might save you a few quid.

Nowadays if you marry a footballer, you're quids in. But before me and Sandra could get married, I had to save up. All the players used to get jobs in those days – even Bobby Moore worked in a factory in Barking for a bit. This Geordie fella called Mr Wilson had a little supermarket on Green Street, just around the corner from West Ham's old ground, Upton Park. I was chatting to him in Porkie's Café one day, mentioned that I was saving up to get married and he offered me a job stacking shelves. Can you imagine someone playing for West Ham nowadays having a part-time job stacking shelves? Even the teenagers are on ten grand a week.

I'd been working at Mr Wilson's for about a week when I popped in to West Ham to pick my wages up. The manager saw me in my white overalls and said, 'Hello, Harry, been doing a bit of painting?'

'No, I've got a part-time job in the supermarket.'

'You can't do that, you're under contract!'

I told him I needed the money for the wedding and he managed to get me another few quid a week.

When I married Sandra, I was getting £25 a week from West Ham and something like £10 a week from coaching kids at schools. I'd get £2.50 – or 50 bob as we'd call it in those days – for three hours every afternoon at Pretoria School in Canning Town. I also worked at Forest Gate County High School and, before that, Harold Road School on Green Street. All the players would go into schools and coach the kids. The manager thought it was a good way for us to spend our time, a good way to improve the kids and it put a few extra quid in our pockets. And remember, that West Ham team included three players who won the World Cup with England: Bobby Moore, Geoff Hurst and Martin Peters. Can you imagine Premier League players going into schools every afternoon to earn a bit of pocket money? But to us, it made perfect sense.

When Sandra was doing her hairdressing apprenticeship, she was on £1.50 a week. When she became the manager, she made £13 a week. Think about that for a moment: in 1967, the manager of a hairdresser's could earn more than half of what a First Division footballer was earning. And I was playing in front of 40,000 people every Saturday. For that to be the case now, a hairdresser might have to be earning a hundred grand a week, and I'm not even sure Vidal Sassoon made that much.

Sandra would come home on a Friday night with the takings, count it out on the table and, if it was a pound short, she'd put a pound of her own money in.

I'd say to her, 'What are you doing?'

'Well, I was a pound short.'

'But that's not your fault!'

'But I'm responsible ... '

I'd have taken a pound out! But that story tells you how honest Sandra is, as well as how much more a pound was worth in those days.

In my playing days, stadiums all over the country would be full every week but that didn't mean all that money was trickling down to the players. Bobby Moore captained England to the World Cup but only would have been on £60 or £70 a week at West Ham. It's unreal when you think about it. And when you go back to before the maximum wage was abolished in 1961, the most a player could earn was £20 a week. Charlton Athletic would be pulling in 60,000 people and some of their players would be paid peanuts.

In those days, we appreciated every little thing we had, because we didn't have a lot. When I was young, we still had rationing, and when my nan got me a Kit-Kat on her ration book, I felt like Charlie Bucket finding a golden ticket. When I left school, one of the first things I did was go to a tailor in Poplar and got myself a mohair suit made to measure. I would only have been earning £6 a week as an apprentice at West Ham, and that first suit would have cost me about £11. I only had a little plastic mac, so one Christmas Eve my dad said he'd buy me a proper overcoat. We went to Burton's in Poplar and they didn't have anything, so we had to walk from

Poplar to Maxi Cohen's in Aldgate, in the freezing cold. When we turned up, all the shops were shutting up, but Maxi's was still open for business. So my dad bought me this magnificent navy blue Crombie, which was so heavy I could hardly walk in it. I must have only been about 10st, so it was like wearing a diver's suit.

But Dad buying me that coat was like winning the pools. And it came in very handy, because I used to have to get the bus every morning to training in Essex, and on matchdays I'd catch a bus to Upton Park. If we had an away game in the early days, I'd have to walk the three miles to Euston or King's Cross, unless Martin Peters drove past and gave me a lift in his Ford Anglia. I loved that coat so much, I couldn't part with it for years. I still had it until recently, when I gave it to my son Mark.

Even if you were skint in those days, that wasn't an excuse not to look good. Every Saturday, we'd all go down the pub in a suit, shirt and tie, and maybe a pair of winkle-picker shoes. We didn't have fights with rockers, but we were basically mods. I wasn't allowed a scooter because I was a footballer, but we all had the mod haircuts and all we spent our money on was clothes.

The most I ever earnt as a footballer was £50 a week, which would have been during my final season at West Ham in 1972. And by that time, I'd been in the first team for seven years. Footballers in my day weren't much different from the man on the street. Most of the West Ham team were from the East End and we never really strayed far from there. Bobby Moore had a nice house in Chigwell, Essex, but that's about as posh as it got. We were part of the community, and our parents wouldn't have stood for us behaving like we were better than everyone else.

There was no such thing as contract negotiations in those days. At the end of the season, you'd make an appointment to see the manager, you'd knock on the door, he'd tell you to sit down and he'd say something like, 'You've done okay this year, Harry, we're going to give you another £2 a week and another two-year contract.' And that was if you were lucky. You'd walk out of the office as happy as a sandboy and when you got home and told the wife, she'd react like you'd won the pools. It wasn't like nowadays, when contract negotiations can last for months. In those days, you signed the piece of paper they put in front of you and that was the end of it. All the players were treated the same, even Bobby Moore.

Which reminds me of a Bobby Moore story. One day, Bobby went in to sign a new contract and when he emerged from the manager's office, Brian Dear was waiting outside. Deary said to Bobby, 'How'd you get on, Bob?' Bobby said, 'Yeah, alright. £100 a week in the season, £40 a week in the summer.'

In goes Deary, and Ron Greenwood says to him, 'I'll give you £40 a week during the season, £30 a week in the summer.'

'Hang on, you've just give Bobby £100 a week during the season and £40 a week in the summer, how can that be right?'

'Well, Bobby's the captain of England. He's in a different class to you.'

'Not in the summer, he ain't!'

Tommy Lawton used to tell a story about his time at Chelsea. At the end of one season, Tommy went to see the manager about his contract. When he walked into the office the manager said, 'Lawton, go back outside, knock on the door and when I say "enter", come back in and stand on that mat over there. When I ask you to approach my desk, approach my desk. When I tell you to sit down, sit down. Do you understand?'

Tommy did as he was told – went outside, knocked on the door, stood on the mat, approached the desk and sat down – and the manager said to him, 'Lawton, you may have scored 30 goals this season, but you could have done better.'

Tommy said he walked out of that office convinced that he'd had a bad season.

Not long after that, in 1947, Tommy transferred from Chelsea to Third Division Notts County for a British transfer record of £20,000. Amazing. Tommy also used to tell the story about the time he was playing for Everton against Manchester City and he had to stand up all the way on the bus to Goodison Park, a journey that took about half an hour. This was a man who scored 38 goals the season Everton won the League title.

When I joined Bournemouth from West Ham, I was their record signing – £31,000. But I was still only on £60 a week, so Sandra used to go round and cut hair. She charged the old girls £1.50 for a shampoo, cut and set. She was pregnant with Jamie at the time but used to lug about one of those bloody great dryers that looked like a space helmet. But we didn't have a choice, because we had no dough. During my short stint at Brentford, I bought an old Morris Marina for £200, but it wouldn't start in the mornings. Sandra was still pregnant, but I'd park on top of a hill and she'd have to give me a push-start. One day, the pet rabbit escaped from its hutch, the dog went after it and the rabbit had a heart attack, while Sandra was pushing me down the road.

When I finished playing in England in 1976, I wanted to buy a taxi, but couldn't afford it. I went to the bank manager and asked if I could borrow money to buy a taxi licence plate. That's just what retired footballers did in those days. They had to get normal jobs, because they came out of football skint. Lots of old footballers bought pubs, and pubs are a good way to lose money. Their mates would come in, expect free drinks, and the following morning they'd discover that the till was half-empty. If a player was a bit more sophisticated, he'd buy a wine bar instead, but the result was usually the same.

Fortunately, I got an offer to play in America for the Seattle Sounders, which got me out of a bit of a fix. Two of my team-mates were Bobby Moore and Geoff Hurst, and the likes of George Best, Pelé and Franz Beckenbauer were among our opponents.

My first job coaching in England was with Bobby Moore. After our time together in Seattle, which included a little stint coaching, he wanted me as his assistant in Oxford. I jumped at the chance, but when I got home I realised he meant Oxford City, who were non-league, rather than Oxford United, who were in the Third Division. They'd come into some money so gave me £90 a week and a little Ford Fiesta with a 950cc engine. I had to drive from Bournemouth to Oxford and back every day, which was almost 200 miles. I didn't last long and neither did Mooro. Come to think of it, neither did the Fiesta.

When I joined Bournemouth as coach, at least it was close to home. But the money was so bad, Sandra had to dust off her scissors. We had two small boys and I was earning less than I did at Oxford. It was only when I got the manager's job that we had any semblance of financial stability. They also threw in a Toyota hatchback, which felt like a Lamborghini compared to the Fiesta.

On average, I reckon people with not a lot of money are just as happy as people with fortunes. Me and Sandra weren't unhappier when I was driving a Morris Marina and she was cutting old ladies' hair for £1.50. And some of the most miserable people I've ever met are rich people. They've got fortunes, but they probably spend most of their time counting their money. They're like a lot of good-looking blokes: they've got no personality and spend too much time staring in the mirror. Not that I've ever suffered from that problem.

20
CRAZY MONEY

'I bought a Bentley and felt
embarrassed ... '

The serious money only started coming into the game when the Premier League kicked off in 1992 and foreign managers started coming to England. Suddenly, the players' wages went through the roof and managers started earning decent dough as well. But with the money came agents, advisors, lawyers, PR experts and someone to hold the player's hairdryer bag, all of them wanting a slice of the deal. And it's true what they say: money corrupts.

In my playing days, you went to a club because you wanted to play for that club, and you stayed there until the manager called you into his office and said, 'I've had an offer for you and I'm letting you go.' I never had an agent – nobody had an agent – and never thought about moving from West Ham until the club wanted rid of me. Now a player goes to a club and his agent is engineering a move as soon as he can, to bring in another big payday.

I recently read a story in the paper about Christian Pulisic's transfer from Borussia Dortmund to Chelsea. A journalist asked Chelsea manager Maurizio Sarri if he'd spoken to Pulisic and Sarri admitted he hadn't. This was days after the deal had been done. And that's how it was for me at the end. I had nothing to do with how much a player earned, bonuses or anything else. I wouldn't even be in the meetings. The first time I'd meet a player was when he turned up for his first day of training. Nowadays, you have teams of recruiters, analysts and all the rest picking a club's players, and agents and lawyers and whoever else making sure their player makes as much money out of the deal as possible. The manager just gets given the players and has to get on with it.

It's all a far cry from my two-minute contract 'negotiations' with Ron Greenwood at West Ham. And it doesn't have much in common with one of my best ever signings, that of Jimmy Case for Bournemouth in 1991. I was watching the local news when a story came on about Jimmy being released by Southampton. Jimmy had won three European Cups with Liverpool, was a Southampton legend and, most importantly, only lived down the road. Hours later, we were having a cup of tea at a service station on the M27. No agent, no lawyer, just me and Jimmy. I offered him £300 a week, he said yes, and that was it. The following season, Jimmy managed to play 40 games for us.

I'm not one for counting my money, I prefer to spend it. I'm a gambler and I also like to help people if I can. As they say, you can't take it with you when you go. But I do have my limits. I bought a Bentley once, and I had it for a month. Someone persuaded me to buy one, but I hated being seen getting in it, hated being seen driving it and hated being seen getting out of it. I just felt embarrassed. I thought that people were looking at me and thinking, 'Who does he think he is?' They probably were. In my head, I'm still that person driving around in a Morris Marina. So I sold the Bentley and lost a fortune.

I've got a Range Rover now, which wasn't cheap, but at least loads of people have got them. Tom Huddlestone, who I had at Tottenham, put me on to them. Tom had four or five cars – he wasn't flash to be fair, he just liked his motors – and one day I said to him, 'Tom, what's your best car?'

'Range Rover.'

'They nice?'

'Fantastic, gaffer, once you've driven one, you'll never want to drive another car.'

So I went out and bought a Range Rover from a place up the road from the Tottenham training ground. I've had one ever since. Oh, and I've also still got that little Ford Focus for the dogs. It stinks, which makes no difference to me because of my gammy nose, but nobody else will go anywhere near it.

I had some big players at West Ham and Portsmouth, but they weren't really flash car people. It was really only when I became manager of Tottenham that I started seeing the training ground fill up with seriously expensive cars. But the first really crazy car I saw was when Spurs signed Emmanuel Adebayor. He had a custom-made black and gold Rolls-Royce, with yellow seats and his initials embroidered into the upholstery. Someone told me it cost over 300 grand. You could probably buy 300,000 Fiestas for that.

Come to think of it, I did have a player at Portsmouth called Sulley Muntari who just about sums up how money and the attitude to it has changed since my playing days. We paid Italian side Udinese about £7 million for Sulley, which was a club record fee at the time. He was a Ghanaian international and was a great player for me, including starting in the 2008 FA Cup final, which we won. Sulley bought a house up the road from me and Sandra in Sandbanks, but he decided he wanted to leave after just one season. He signed for Inter Milan, and when he upped sticks and moved to Italy, he left his Mercedes in the drive. I just assumed he'd sold the house or he'd come back at some point and do it up, but he just left it to go to rack and ruin. The garden was all overgrown, plants were climbing up the windows, and the Mercedes had gone all rusty and rotten. The house was only sold recently, ten years after he left.

Sulley had a fleet of cars, including a six-wheeled Merc that cost almost a million quid. And I remember reading a story about him handing out money to slum kids when he was playing in the World Cup in Brazil. At the time, he was playing for AC Milan. But a couple of years back, Sulley had another Merc seized off him by the Italian police. Apparently, he had fallen behind with his payments. Incredible. Sulley played for some of the biggest teams in Europe, in two World Cups and won the Champions League with Inter. Can you imagine growing up poor in Africa and suddenly being on

50 grand a week? I'm sure lads like Sulley enjoy it, but it must be difficult for them in other ways.

But players going skint is more common than you might imagine. Even when I was playing, some of the gambling on the coach could get out of control. A player could do a week's wages on a game of cards, easy. But that was when a week's wages was only about 50 quid, so God knows how much they must play for now. I knew one player who was doing 50-grand greyhound forecasts. One afternoon, he was up £1.5 million, but by the end of the night, he was £1.5 million down. And I knew of another player who was losing anything between 150 and 200 grand a day.

But gambling is only part of it. Players get used to the high life and when they retire, they carry on buying big houses and expensive cars. They have girlfriends and wives who have become accustomed to a certain standard of living, and kids in posh public schools. But there's no money to feed that lifestyle anymore. It just goes to show, money is all relative. I always tell young players, 'Buy property rather than cars.' That's the game to be in, like Frank Lampard Jr and former Liverpool striker Robbie Fowler, who own property all over the place. Robbie owns about half of England.

I don't think modern footballers are looked after very well. There are one or two agents that are okay, I'm sure. But there are an awful lot of them who aren't interested in the players as people and see them purely as money-making machines. It happens to a lot of players. Their agents, who players think are their pals, get them to invest in all sorts of schemes and plans, most of which they have a personal involvement in and from which they stand to earn commission. And when the player hangs up his boots, the agent scurries off, never to be seen again. And it's when a player retires that he needs help most.

Sometimes I think back to my nan, sitting out on the street of an evening, chatting with the other old girls and drinking tea. Nobody in the East End owned anything of any value, so nobody was sad about not having anything. Instead of looking over the garden fence and wanting what their neighbours had, they'd lean on the garden fence and have a chat for an hour. Life was simpler back then and, on the whole, people were happier for it.

21
FANDOM

'Besty might be shagging your
old woman ...'

I find it strange when people support teams from the other end of
the country. I suppose kids want to support a team that's winning.
Or they'll watch a game on the telly, pick out a favourite player
and whoever he plays for will be their team. But I think if you're
from Newcastle, you should support Newcastle. Or if you're from
Norwich, you should support Norwich. But whoever you support
and however passionate you are about something, you need to
show respect.

It's great where I live now: most of the kids seem to support
Bournemouth, and that wasn't always the case. And when I was at

Portsmouth, you didn't often see people walking about in Chelsea or Arsenal shirts. Portsmouth was their city and their team. It's always been a bit different in London, where there are loads of teams. In the East End, most people have always supported West Ham. But how many proper football fans live in Chelsea? Even my dad supported Arsenal.

There wasn't much hooliganism when I was growing up. My dad would put a suit and tie on for some games and I'd take a rattle. If you tried to take a rattle into a ground nowadays, they'd confiscate it at the turnstile, because they'd think you wanted to wrap it round somebody's head. But Millwall's Den was always quite intimidating. One Christmas, my dad got chinned and ended up with his jaw wired up, so he couldn't eat his Christmas dinner.

But football supporters were a different breed in those days. There wasn't the same nastiness there is now. Supporters desperately wanted us to win every week and would get the hump if we lost or didn't play well, but the atmosphere would never be toxic. If you had a bad game, they'd give you a bit of grief, but it would be a laugh, good-natured banter. It was the same in the crowd. I remember when Notts Forest and England goalkeeper Peter Shilton got caught with a woman in his car who wasn't his wife. It was all over the newspapers on Saturday morning, and when he ran out at Anfield later that afternoon, all the Liverpool fans were singing, 'Who were you with last night?'

I briefly played with George Best at Bournemouth in the early 1980s, when neither of us were at our peaks. He only played about a dozen games, but he did a deal which meant he got a share of the gate money. That was fair enough because, when he played, he trebled the crowd.

I loved Besty, he was a fantastic fella. One morning he rang me and asked if I wanted to go to Salisbury races with him. I picked up him and his girlfriend – the former Miss World Mary Stävin – and after I dropped her off at the station, George turned to me and said, 'Thank God she's gone, she's been driving me mad. We went to the pictures last night and she wouldn't stop kissing me and biting my neck.'

I said to him, 'Sounds terrible, George . . . '

On the way home from the racecourse, George spotted two blokes walking along the road. He said to me, 'They look like they've done their dough, let's give them a lift.' They both jumped in and George chatted to them all the way to Fordingbridge.

George wasn't really focused on football. One week, he didn't turn up for our game in Bradford. Bournemouth's managing director Brian Tiler went down to London to try to find him and George's girlfriend Mary gave Brian a list of pubs he might be in. Eventually, Brian tracked George down in some boozer and said to him, 'Come on, George, you've got to play tomorrow, the boys will want you there.' George nodded along for a bit before going to the toilet and climbing out of the window.

That Saturday, I was on the bench at Valley Parade and as I was warming up, this Bradford fan said to me, ''Ere, Redknapp, where's Besty?'

'I dunno.'

'Well, you wanna be more careful, he might be round your house shagging your old woman.'

When I started going to watch football, me and my dad would get there two hours early and take our regular place behind the goal. I'd stand on a big manhole cover that stuck up about a foot off the ground, so that I could see. There was no segregation in the 1950s, the fans all mixed together. You just walked in, bought a ticket and stood wherever you liked. If we were playing Bolton, for example, my dad would get chatting to a couple of their fans, ask them how their journey was and offer them some tea from his flask. And when the game started, you cheered your team instead of abusing the opposition.

At West Ham, the whole of the Chicken Run would belt out 'Bubbles' – 'I'm forever blowing bubbles, pretty bubbles in the air!' – over and over again. That was one of the greatest sights and sounds in football: the whole ground packed, everyone swaying and singing in harmony. If I close my eyes now and think about, it's like I'm almost back there on the pitch. To be fair, they still sing 'Bubbles' over at the London Stadium, where West Ham have moved to, but it all seems quite quaint and old-fashioned compared to some of the other stuff they come out with.

The hooliganism really kicked in during the late 1960s. We'd be on a train coming back from a game in Manchester or wherever, we'd stop at a station and suddenly a load of nutters would jump on and start fighting our fans. They'd be rolling about in the carriages, swinging bottles around their heads and spilling out onto the platform.

I remember returning from my spell in America and going to watch Millwall play West Ham at Upton Park. As anyone who knows anything about English football will be aware, Millwall and West Ham fans don't get on very well. There were loads of skinheads marching down the street, wearing bovver boots and rolled-up jeans, and everyone was throwing bottles and bricks at each other. In Seattle, fans would have tailgate parties next to the ground and share a couple of beers and a hamburger.

How that Chicken Run never collapsed or went up in flames I'll never know. It was made of wood, and everyone would smoke, flick their butts on the floor and jump up and down for 90 minutes. You'd look underneath and there would be newspapers, programmes, cigarette packets and fag ends piled about eight feet high, so that the rubbish almost touched the bottom of the steps. Of course, it was the Bradford City stadium fire in 1985 and the Hillsborough disaster four years later that changed everything.

The 1970s and '80s were a dangerous time to watch football, but even when hooliganism was at its height, the singing and chanting was never like it is now. One of the ironies of modern football for me is that as the stadiums have got nicer and the hooliganism has died down, the abuse from the fans has got filthier.

I sympathise with football fans, because the cost to watch it nowadays is astronomical. If you're taking the kids, you're talking hundreds of pounds for the day, including tickets, travel, food and drinks. When I was a kid, it was a couple of shillings to stand and maybe five bob for a seat, which translates to about five or six quid in today's money. It doesn't need to be so expensive for fans, because the clubs get so much TV money that the gate money doesn't even make that much difference to them, at least in the Premier League. So the clubs could do something about it, but instead they pay crazy wages to players. So you get people who say, 'We pay our money, we're entitled to say what we like.' But there's no excuse for vile behaviour, however much you're paying to get in. As well as being mystified by people drinking champagne rather than Bovril, the fans who swayed and sang 'Bubbles' in the old Chicken Run would turn in their graves if they heard the sort of stuff West Ham fans come out with nowadays. And not just West Ham fans, but fans of a lot of clubs.

After the Munich air disaster in 1958, the whole country mourned. Every morning at school we'd say prayers for the players that were in hospital. Fast forward 30 years, and opposition fans were singing sick songs about the disaster to the Man Utd fans. And then you get Man Utd fans singing sick songs to Liverpool fans about the Hillsborough disaster. It used to make me ill when I heard stuff like that. After the Argentinian player Emiliano Sala died in a plane crash recently, Southampton fans were doing aeroplane gestures to the Cardiff fans. Those kinds of idiots are just as bad as the people who shout racist remarks. I've never been able to comprehend that sort of behaviour, other than to say they must be morons, or don't have any brains at all.

I couldn't believe it when West Ham fans threw bottles at the Man Utd coach before the final game at Upton Park in 2016. It wasn't even as if it was one or two of them, there were quite a few of them. That was meant to be a night of celebration and reminiscing about all the great games at Upton Park and the great players who graced that ground. But how is throwing bottles at the opposition's coach celebrating anything? They can't be proper football fans, simply because proper football fans wouldn't do that. All these filthy signs they make to opposition players and managers, what's that all about? I assume they think abusing people intimidates them. But the best way of intimidating the opposition is by getting behind your own team. When I heard 'Bubbles' being sung at Upton Park, I'd feel ten-feet tall and want to run through walls for them.

The first time I remember a player getting really vile abuse was when Ronny Rosenthal was playing for Tottenham in the mid-1990s. Ronny was Jewish, and some of the stuff opposition fans came out with was shocking. Some of the abuse Sol Campbell got from Tottenham fans, after he left them for north London rivals Arsenal, was just as bad. And the way Frank Lampard Jr was treated by West Ham fans after he left for Chelsea was terrible. I could never understand it. He was great for West Ham for a few years, but after me and his dad left, he was hardly going to stick around. And Chelsea paid very good money for him.

When I was managing Portsmouth, I got into a row with some Aston Villa fans who were shouting filth at me. There were little kids calling me all the names under the sun. I didn't bring my kids up to talk like that and I shouldn't have to stand there and take it. In the same game, someone threw a coin that hit the linesman on the head. I think they were probably aiming at me, but I didn't think I deserved it either. Other times I'd see dads, and even mums, shouting abuse and making filthy signs while their son or daughter was by their side. Maybe I shouldn't have let it upset me, but it did.

When I left Portsmouth to manage south coast rivals Southampton, I had no idea the ructions it would cause. But fans don't know what's going on behind the scenes. Portsmouth's owner Milan Mandarić decided he wanted to bring in a director of football, even though he already had me and my assistant Jim Smith, who was about 100 at the time, so it wasn't as if we were lacking the experience. Anyway, Milan brought this Croatian chap in and I left. I had no intention of going to Southampton, but their chairman Rupert Lowe contacted me and, because I had no idea how much Southampton and Portsmouth fans hated each other, I took the job.

That was a nightmare time for me, because those Pompey fans don't mess around. The first morning I turned up at Southampton's training ground, there were banners outside with 'JUDAS' and 'SCUM' written on them. It turned out the boys doing the roadworks were Portsmouth fans. Some of the stuff they said to me I wouldn't like to repeat. I got it from all angles. I'd be out in the garden and I'd hear people screaming all sorts of abuse. Sandra would hear it, too, and it would scare her. We got phone calls in the middle of the night, people saying they hoped I got cancer or turned my car over and killed my wife. These people aren't human beings. I genuinely feel sorry for them.

When Southampton played Portsmouth, we had four former SAS men on the coach, helicopters hovering overhead and police on every bridge. The poor players didn't have a clue what was going on. I don't mind a bit of aggro, but I've never understood why there would be so much nastiness between different clubs. My team were so scared, we went 3–0 down in no time and ended up losing 4–1. I obviously still knew most of the Portsmouth lads, and I swear they stopped scoring more goals deliberately. I don't think I left the bench the whole game. I just couldn't wait to get out of there.

It was the same after I left Portsmouth second time around for Tottenham, and that was after we'd won the FA Cup for the first time in almost 70 years and qualified for Europe for the first time. I felt I'd gone as far as I could with Portsmouth, so when I got the chance to manage Spurs, I didn't think I could turn it down.

That offer came completely out of the blue. We were travelling back from Braga in Portugal and I was sat next to Portsmouth's chief executive, Peter Storrie. My phone went and when I answered, it was Tottenham chairman Daniel Levy on the other end. Daniel said, 'Harry, we want you to be our manager, can we meet?' It was obviously a bit awkward, what with Peter being sat next to me.

When I got off the phone, Peter said to me, 'Who was that?', and I said, 'I dunno, couldn't hear properly, probably a wrong number ... '

That night, I went and met Daniel and he made a formal offer. Three days later, I was receiving the freedom of the city of Portsmouth. My timing has never been very good. As you can imagine, I got a lovely welcome. When I walked on the stage at the Guildhall, people were booing me, calling me Judas and wearing T-shirts that said, 'Rot in Hell'.

Then there are the fans who think they know more than the manager, which is almost all of them. When I was at West Ham, me and Frank Lampard Jr attended a fans' forum and this fan started telling me Frank wasn't good enough to play for the club. We'd just let a kid called Scott Canham go to Brentford, and this bloke was telling me he was better than Frank. Fans have a right to an opinion, but as a manager, it's my job to make decisions. So I put this fan right. I told him, 'There will be no comparison between what Frank Lampard and Scott Canham achieve in football. Frank will go right to the very top.' I got a round of applause for that, so some of the fans saw things the same as me.

I should say that the vast majority of fans have been good as gold to me over the years. I had ten years at Bournemouth and they loved me. I'm always treated well by West Ham and Tottenham fans, and I get on great with most Portsmouth fans with any sense. I even got on alright with fans of QPR, because even though we got relegated that first season, we were rock bottom when I joined, and I got them back up the following year.

Time for one last story about mad fans. One year, I took West Ham to Oxford City for a pre-season friendly. There was this hardcore Hammers fan behind the dugout, with a skinhead and covered in West Ham tattoos. And even before we'd kicked off, he was getting into my ear: ''Arry, please tell me we 'aven't got that Lee Chapman up front again this year? Why don't you go out and buy a decent striker?' All first half he was going on about Lee Chapman, he would not leave me alone.

At half-time, I made five substitutions, but two minutes into the second half, we had an injury, which left us with only ten men. This fan was still shouting at me, so I turned to him and said, 'Oi! Can you play as good as you talk?'

'I'm better than that Chapman.'

'Come on then, get your gear on and we'll have a look at you.'

'What do you mean?'

'You're playing.'

'Who for?'

'West Ham.'

'I ain't got no boots.'

'What size are you?'

'Nine.'

'Eddie, get him a pair of boots ... '

Eddie the kitman took this bloke into the changing room and he came out in football boots and a full West Ham kit. He asked me where I wanted him to play, and I replied, 'Go up front, I want to see if you're better than Chapman.' So he waddled on, his feet facing in different directions, and the Tannoy announcer ran up to me, wanting to know who he was.

'Harry, who's number 16?'

'Who's number 16? Ain't you been watching the World Cup? Chichichaev, the Bulgarian striker.'

'I thought it was him ... '

Anyway, this bloke only went and scored. And I've got to be honest, he was better than Chapman, at least on the night. But that's what supporting a football team should be about: having fun, rather than being horrible.

22
ADVERSITY

'I'd get so low it was scary . . . '

When I was managing and we won, the high would be unbelievable. I'd be in the car driving home on my own, punching the air and screaming, 'Fuckin' yes! Get in there!' People must have been driving past thinking, 'Is this geezer mad or what?' But as a football manager, you never get to enjoy a win for long. So a couple of hours after a win, I'd already be thinking about the next game. Even the most wonderful of lives will contain their fair share of adversity.

I recently bumped into the golf commentator Peter Alliss, and he said to me, 'Harry, either you've got a bloody good hairdresser or you've had no stress in your life.' He was referring to the fact I've still got my hair and none of it's gone grey. Until recently, Sandra always cut my hair (I went to the barber the other day and thought it would still be two and sixpence), so Peter was right about the first bit. But believe me, I've had plenty of stress in my life.

As a football manager, there's always that pressure to win every game, because you know that if you go four or five games without winning, the vultures will start circling. It's not a sane occupation, which is why so many players and managers have silly superstitions. If my team were winning, I'd carry on wearing the same blazer, trousers and tie until we lost. When I was at Bournemouth, we went about 20 games unbeaten and, in the end, my gear was walking to the ground on its own. But as a manager, you've got to be realistic. You know you're not going to win the League if you're manager of Bournemouth, or even West Ham. Not unless a new owner comes along and gives you £500 million to spend on players, or you have a miracle like Leicester. But when my team lost, I'd get so low it was scary. I'd sink into a deep depression which was really quite dangerous. It was like someone in the family had died.

Sometimes, my mate Clive would come with me and if we'd been beat, he'd know not to waste his time talking to me on the way home. And, like most managers, I couldn't help taking it into the house with me. Next time you see a manager being interviewed after a defeat, look closely at his face and it will tell you exactly what kind of weekend him and his family have got to look forward to. Most managers are miserable gits. I certainly was. The highs were like nothing else I've ever experienced, but I don't miss those lows. If my team lost just before Christmas, it wouldn't be a happy Christmas Day for me.

Sandra could never make arrangements to go out with anyone else after a game, because she knew that if we'd lost, I'd have the raving hump. Sometimes she'd say to me during the week, 'So and so has asked us to go out with them next Saturday.' And I'd have to say, 'We can't. If we don't win, I'll be no use.' I just wouldn't want to see or talk to anybody. Sandra knew it would take me a day or two to recover. She'd cook me pasta and maybe open a bottle of wine and just wait for me to come round. Sometimes, I'd have to drink Night Nurse before going to bed, to help me sleep. Even then, I'd be awake and staring at the ceiling at one o'clock in the morning, my mind racing. I just wouldn't be able to pull myself out of it until maybe late on Sunday, because there was no point turning up to training on Monday with a face like thunder.

A manager has support staff, but it's still a lonely business. As a manager, the buck stops with you. When you're a coach, you'll take the training, everybody has fun and everybody likes you. But there's not much that's fun about being a manager. You're picking the team, which means some players you leave out will hate you. If you lose, not only will the fans hate you, your wife, kids, mum and dad will hate you, because you'll be insufferable.

Managers get stuck in front of a TV camera and have a microphone stuck up their nose just after their team's been beat and played rubbish. That's the toughest bit of all, an absolute nightmare. Some managers will come on and talk a load of crap: 'Well, we got beat 5–0, but there were a lot of positives to take from the game.' I'll be watching it and thinking, 'Really? Show me one, because I didn't see any.' When I was interviewed, I couldn't help but say it how it was. If we were rubbish, I'd say we were rubbish. There was no point saying any different. And on Monday morning, you'd have to go back into training and start all over again. Fans might see you and start complaining about the result and the performance, and the chairman would have the hump with you, be moaning that he'd spent all his money on the team for nothing.

But the pressure didn't really come directly from the chairman, the board, the players or the fans. The pressure came from within. It was the sense of responsibility that laid me so low. I felt responsible for the club, the people at the club and the fans who paid their money to watch us play. As a manager, I was ultimately responsible for the performances of the club they loved. I was always worrying about other people's problems. Football managers are also agony aunts and fixers. Players would come to me with problems with their girlfriends or wives, problems with gambling or boozing, problems with their dog, problems with not getting paid as much as their team-mates. And if things weren't going well, all that responsibility would weight more heavily on my shoulders. I'd feel like I'd let everybody down. You don't want to be the manager of a club like West Ham when you're getting beat all the time. You don't want to be seen anywhere, certainly not anywhere in east London.

Football management at the highest level is a great job, and a well-paid job, but I wouldn't say it was enjoyable. One season, West Ham were in a spot of bother and we needed Middlesbrough to get a win to help us out. I couldn't face watching Boro's game on the telly, so me and Frank Lampard Sr went out for a bite to eat. But we never made it to the restaurant. Instead, we phoned up Middlesbrough ClubCall and spent the whole game passing the phone between us while sitting in the car. And look at Arsène

Wenger. When he first joined Arsenal, I remember reading articles saying that he was like a professor, that he'd just sit and study the game, while other managers were screaming and shouting and behaving like idiots. The thing was, he didn't lose many games back then. When his team did start losing, Arsène started screaming and hollering and kicking things. He ended up being as bad as everyone else.

And it's arguably even less enjoyable for the lads in the lower divisions. They come out of football, maybe get a job as a coach somewhere, before moving into management if they're lucky. And the whole time they know that if they lose that job, that could be it, they might not find a management job elsewhere. I've been there, so I know. When I started managing Bournemouth, I was in my mid-30s with a couple of young kids, not much money and a car that needed pushing. That's pressure.

How many managers make it to the top? Not many. Look at Bobby Moore. Mooro was one of the greatest players England ever produced but he took jobs at Oxford City and Southend, clubs with no money and no players. He was immediately written off as a manager, but I still maintain he could have been the greatest manager West Ham ever had.

And it's especially tough for British managers nowadays: out of 20 teams in the Premier League, only five managers are home-grown, and that trend has even started trickling down to the lower divisions. And if ex-players can't carve out a career in management, what are they going to do with their lives? They've been playing football since they were a kid, they've got no expertise in anything else and they're still only in their 30s. That's why you get so many lads who get very, very low when they finish playing. It's not just that they miss the buzz, but also because they're lost.

It hasn't just been the football and Sandra's health issues that have made me stressed. The court case for tax evasion was hanging over me for five years and was horrendous. Five years is a lot of time to think about how things might turn out. Would I end up in prison? Without Sandra, my sons and my grandchildren? And when the trial finally came around, I'd think some strange things: 'What if everyone on the jury hates Tottenham? What if they're all Arsenal fans? What if the bloke in my prison cell is an Arsenal fan?'

The nightmare started in November 2007. I was on my way home from Germany, where I'd been watching Glasgow Rangers play Stuttgart, because I thought Stuttgart's centre-half might be able to do a job for Portsmouth. When I got off the plane, I turned on my phone and had a load of missed calls and voicemails from Sandra, who was in a terrible state. When I finally made contact, she told me that the police had stormed our house at six o'clock in the morning, when it was still dark. Photographers from the *Sun* had even come along for the ride, although the police denied tipping them off. Sandra's immediate thought was that I'd been involved in a plane crash, because why else would the police and photographers be swarming all over the house at 6am?

I have no idea why the police thought they had to be so heavy-handed, other than that they thought I was some East End gangster who might pull out a sawn-off shotgun. They could have just asked me to come in for an interview. And all they got for their troubles was a computer that I'd bought for Sandra a couple of Christmases earlier, which had never even been switched on.

When I reported to Chichester police station, they stuck me in a police cell. That was the first time I'd ever been in one. And all I could think was, 'What would my mum and dad think if they could see me in here?' They were good, honest people. And I wasn't crooked either. If anything, I was too soft. If someone says there's a little boy in hospital somewhere, or anyone else in a difficult situation, I'll do what I can to help. I feel I have a responsibility to help others less fortunate than me. I'm lucky enough to be in a privileged position where I can help, and I enjoy it. So I didn't know what I'd done to deserve being in the dock, and it was scary finding myself in that situation.

When I joined Portsmouth in 2001, it was as director of football, looking after player recruitment. At the time, Milan said to me, 'Harry, I can't pay you as much as West Ham were paying you, but if you bring in a player and sell them on for a profit, you'll receive 10 per cent of that.' A week or so later, we bought Peter Crouch from QPR for £1.25 million. Nine months later, we sold him for £4.5 million. The problem was, I was now Portsmouth manager and hadn't noticed that my new contract no longer contained the 10 per cent profit clause.

Milan refused to pay me the 10 per cent bonus for Crouch's sale, and I had the hump. But to keep me happy, Milan instead promised to buy some shares and give me the profits from those. I wasn't happy with the arrangement, I just wanted the bonus from the Crouch deal. But in the end, I realised Milan wasn't going to give it to me, so I took Sandra with me to Monaco, met Milan's bank manager and opened an account. The bank manager asked me for a password, and I chose Rosie47, which was a combination of the name of my dog at the time and my year of birth. There wasn't even any money in the account at the time, and I doubted there ever would be.

I forgot about the account until a couple of years later. Portsmouth had won at Blackburn to stay in the Premier League for a second season and Milan was kissing and cuddling me in the boardroom and telling me how much he loved me. So I thought it would be a good time to ask him about the account in Monaco.

'Any luck with those shares you bought for me, Milan?'

'Rubbish! Rubbish! I lost millions! But don't worry, Harry, I'll put some more money in and hopefully it will be different ... '

When I told my assistant Jim Smith about the conversation with Milan, he said, 'Harry, are you mad? He's wound you up, he never put any money in in the first place.'

Not long after that, Milan told me he'd made some more investments and that they'd bombed again. I told my accountant about this account in Monaco and he managed to track it down. It turned out there was a bit of money in there, which my accountant drew out. When I told him that the money wasn't mine and belonged to Milan, my accountant replied, 'Well, he's done you for the Peter Crouch bonus, let him ask for his money back.'

In 2006, I'd been interviewed about corruption in football, along with every other manager in the Premier League. They asked me where I banked and I replied, 'HSBC. I do have another account in Monaco, but I don't know the name of the bank. When you interview the chairman, ask him, he knows the details.'

This anti-corruption team were investigating the transfer of Amdy Faye, and specifically about a payment of £100,000 to Faye's agent, Willie McKay, which they suspected had been made to avoid tax. They wanted to know who had authorised the payment, and I told them what I've already told you, that managers have got nothing to do with that side of the game. All I did was coach the players and pick the team, and the anti-corruption team accepted that. But then the police suddenly got involved and thought it would be a good idea to scare the life out of Sandra.

Not only did the police seem to think I was some sort of east London villain, they also seemed to think I was a criminal mastermind, shifting my money all over Europe in order to avoid paying tax. The truth was very different. I'm a mug with money. My mum and dad kept any money they had in a biscuit tin. Sandra does everything for me, and she was a hairdresser, not the Chancellor of the Exchequer. It was only when my accountant started going through my finances that I realised the *Sun* hadn't paid me for my column for 18 months. But the police and HMRC were now trying to nail me over this mystery bank account in Monaco and suddenly I was in court, knowing that if I got found guilty, I'd be going away for three years.

As it turned out, Milan was amazing in court. When the prosecuting QC suggested Milan had got me to open an account in Monaco so that he could pay me offshore and avoid paying tax, Milan replied, 'Mr Black, I woke up one morning and said to my friend Harry: "Harry, I'm bored, let's go and break the law today, do something exciting. I have paid £9 million in income tax so far this year, but let's go to Monaco and see if we can avoid paying £12,000 on a bonus." Mr Black, do you really think this is true?'

At one time, Milan employed something like 40,000 people in Silicon Valley and his company was the largest manufacturer of computer components in America. When I was playing over there, he owned the San José Earthquakes, which was the richest team apart from New York Cosmos, who were owned by Warner Communications. So Milan's testimony was very convincing, and I could tell it won over members of the jury. But it was my first time in the dock and I didn't cope with it as well as Milan.

I wouldn't let Sandra come to court, I'd have cried all day seeing her sitting there. But Jamie came every day, and stayed with me in my hotel at night, while Mark stayed at home with his mum. It was a long, drawn-out affair, and I was managing Tottenham at the time. During the trial, we played Liverpool away, and they adjourned a little bit early so I could catch a private plane from London City Airport. We dashed to the airport, jumped on the plane, the plane took off and suddenly they announced there was a problem and we'd have to come back down again. They couldn't fix it, so I had to watch the game on TV. Thankfully, we got a draw. Another night, Tottenham played Newcastle and we were 4–0 up at half-time. And every time we scored, I jumped as high as the ceiling. It was the release of all that pent-up emotion.

I was very lucky that I had very good barrister in John Kelsey Fry, who exuded charisma and is an absolute genius. It was a pleasure to watch him work and he secured me the verdict I so desperately wanted to hear: not guilty. Not that I did much celebrating. I skipped the gathering of friends and supporters back at the hotel and drove straight back down south to see Sandra. I was in bed by nine o'clock, because I had barely slept for 15 days.

I also had a couple of very low points with Tottenham. The first was the time Chelsea beat Bayern Munich in the final of the Champions League in 2012, which meant they qualified for the following year's tournament instead of us. I went to see that game in Germany, and it turned out to be a terrible night. Then there was losing my job a couple of months later, despite the fact we'd just finished fourth in the League. Nobody bothered telling me why.

When I was at Southampton, I barely slept for weeks. My assistant Jim Smith used to actually say to me, 'Harry, this job will kill you.' I just felt under so much pressure to keep Southampton up. And when I left Portsmouth for a second time, I made up my mind to jack it all in. But I decided to carry on. It wasn't about the money. I could afford to live without football, but I couldn't actually live without football, however unhappy it was making me.

But I never look back when things don't go to plan. When I didn't get the England job, I didn't go and lie down in a dark room and sulk about it. That's just life, everyone has good days and bad days. We all get the hump about things, whether you're a football manager or work in an office. And there are far worse things going on in the world. What else can you do but move on? After I lost my job at Tottenham, I thought, 'If I have to play golf every day for the rest of my life, that's what I'll do.' Then I injured my knee and I couldn't do that either.

There's actually a funny story tied to being sacked by Tottenham and not hired by England. Just before they made the England announcement, a boy in the local golf shop gave me a present, but told me not to open it until he told me. When I didn't get the England job, he rung me up and said, 'Don't open that box, I've got another one for you.' About two months later, he brought the other box round, and that was the day I lost my job at Tottenham. It turned out the first box had contained a pair of England shoes, and the second box had contained a pair of Tottenham shoes. So I said to him, 'Look, I'll give you ten grand not to buy me another pair of shoes.' He did buy me a pair of QPR shoes, although I left of my own accord, so it wasn't a problem.

You get people who think that players and managers aren't allowed to be low or depressed because they've got lots of money. But just because you've got money doesn't necessarily mean you're going to be happy. You can be depressed because the side's not doing well, you're not in the team, you're homesick, you've got problems with your relationship, or you're simply suffering with mental illness. So many things in life can get you low, and getting low doesn't mean you're weak – it just means you're human.

23
KIDS' STUFF

'If you're good enough, you're old enough ... '

Nowadays, big clubs sign kids, often schoolboy stars, and they disappear, sometimes forever. They play youth football for three or four years, never get anywhere near the first team, and often fade into obscurity. My son Jamie was wise enough to know that playing proper men's football at the age of 16 would be far better for him in the grand scheme of things. Why would you want to be playing with other kids on a training ground with no one there, instead of playing meaningful matches with and against men, where there are points at stake, thousands of fans and real pressure to perform? I've always believed that if you're good enough, you're old enough.

And that goes for anything, whether you're a budding footballer or a kid who plays the violin.

I went to West Ham when I was 15 and suddenly I was playing in front of 25,000 people in FA Youth Cup games. Months earlier, I'd been playing on cinder pitches at school in front of a man and his dog, if we were lucky. In those days, a club's youth team was a big deal, but now they don't even play youth games in stadiums. And reserve team football also meant something back then. On a Friday, the manager would put four team sheets up: first team, reserves, A team and youth team. Because you were only allowed one substitution per game anyway, most people missed out on the first team. But that meant the reserves would be made up of eight senior players and a few kids, so the kids were playing proper football with proper players. That's how you learnt the game in those days.

Nowadays, academy kids don't mix with first team players. But when I was at Tottenham, the first club to show an interest in me, I'd sit on the touchline at their training ground in Cheshunt and watch the first team go through their repertoire of tricks. This was the side that won the League and Cup double in 1960–61, with legendary players like Danny Blanchflower, Dave Mackay, Cliff Jones and John White.

At West Ham, the manager Ron Greenwood would always watch the youth team play. Mr Greenwood, as us kids had to call him, was quite a formal person – it's not as if you'd be able to have a laugh and a joke with him in his office. But he was an amazing coach and a very good people person. He really cared about the kids because he considered them to be the club's future. The year we won the FA Youth Cup in 1963, Ron came to watch us play Wolves in the semi-final first leg at Molineux instead of the first team game. Imagine Manchester City manager Pep Guardiola going to watch the kids instead of a Premier League game. And it wasn't just Ron who showed a keen interest. At the second leg at Upton Park, the whole first team were up in the stands watching.

Bobby Moore and the lads would also have been up in the stands when we beat Liverpool 5–2 in the second leg of the FA Youth Cup final, to win 6–5 on aggregate. We had three 15-year-olds in our team, which was unheard of, and Martin Britt, our big centre-forward, scored four goals. So when I was a 17-year-old at West Ham, I considered Bobby Moore to be a good pal of mine. When I played my first senior game in 1965, I didn't feel intimidated, because I'd been mixing with the players for years, so I already knew everyone. And this mixing of youth with experience is one of the reasons we had a conveyor belt of players coming out of the youth team and straight into the first team. A few days before my debut for the first team against Sunderland, I was playing in the South East Counties side against Chelsea. For a local boy playing in front of 40,000 people under floodlights at Upton Park was incredible, but I felt ready for it.

Nowadays, reserve football is beneath a lot of players. Towards the end of my management career, it was murder trying to get people to play in the reserves, even if they'd been out injured for months:

'You need to play.'

'Nah, I'll get fit in training.'

'Have a game in the reserves.'

'I don't want to play in the reserves … '

They just didn't see the benefit. But when I played in the reserves and we were at home, 10,000 might turn up to watch us play, maybe because they couldn't afford or didn't have time to go and watch the first team in Newcastle or wherever. As we were playing, we'd hear the first team score being announced on the Tannoy – 'Liverpool 0, West Ham 1' – and the crowd would go mad. It all made sense, because the kids would not only be getting a taste of men's football, they'd be getting a taste of the atmosphere and pressure involved in football at the highest level. It was a better way of learning the game than coaching, that's for sure, but it doesn't happen anymore.

Even the youngsters don't play reserve football these days, because they play under-21 and under-23 football instead – which is not proper football. If you haven't made it by that age, you might as well forget it. And you watch this under-23s football and everyone is strolling about and passing it. That's all they do, pass, pass, pass, and nobody ever puts a proper tackle in.

That's why I used to loan my kids out when I was at West Ham. Lampard went to Swansea, where he played in ankle-deep mud at the Vetch Field. I'd go and watch him play, to see how he was coping getting booted all over the pitch by old veterans from Rochdale or Stockport County. And that's how he got better. Michael Carrick went to Swindon, Rio Ferdinand and Jermain Defoe went to Bournemouth, Glen Johnson went to Millwall. The only one I didn't loan out was Joe Cole, because he was already on the verge of the first team at 16.

Those that went out on loan came back as different players and different people. Instead of being pampered at their Premier League club, they had to stand on their own two feet. They would be training with players in their 30s, people who had been in the game for 20 years, who they could talk to and learn from. And they would be playing against experienced pros, who would think nothing about steaming into them or sticking an elbow in their face. Winning youth cups is one thing, but getting into the first team at Man City or Chelsea is something else completely. Chelsea have won the FA Youth Cup for six of the last seven years, but how many of those players have graduated to the first team? Hardly any. And I think one of the reasons is because these kids aren't learning how to play real football – men's football – early enough.

I'm still a big believer in the loan system, but they've made it difficult for the smaller teams. Now, when you take a player on loan, you have to pay a loan fee. So if I'm managing Brentford and I want to take a player from Chelsea or Tottenham, I might have to pay anywhere between £500,000 and £1 million for the season. That's on top of the player's wages. And if he doesn't play, I have to pay double his wages as a forfeit. So if this player turns up and is no good or a bit of a tosser around the place, I'm stuck with him regardless. It's farcical. You're talking about mega-rich clubs, who are already making fortunes off the Premier League, ripping off clubs lower down the food chain who are struggling to survive. It's no longer a case of their young players learning to play the game, it's all about making more money.

Most managers at the top level don't watch their youth teams play anymore. But when I was managing West Ham, me and my assistant Frank Lampard Sr would watch the kids all the time. We'd finish training the first team and go and watch the youth teams for an hour. We'd also watch youth matches on a Sunday morning, so we knew if any decent kids were coming through. In a lot of cases, the kids don't even train at the same place as the first team nowadays. A club's academy will be miles down the road. In my day, the kids would be training on the next pitch, so if we had any injuries in training, or we needed a couple of extra players for a full-scale practice match, we'd call some kids over.

There's such a wastage of young talent in this country. I'll watch these amazing kids at 11 or 12 and they'll just disappear. What happens to them all? I think one of the reasons is that, too often, nobody pays enough attention to them. There's not enough one-on-one work, they're all just all lumped together. That's not right, because every kid is different. And I'm not just talking about one-on-one football coaching, I'm talking about one-on-one chats, finding out what makes them tick, what problems they might have and teaching them about life. These kids join academies when they're six or seven, and so few of them make the grade. And when they get chucked on the scrapheap, they don't know anything else.

When I was an apprentice, I had jobs to do apart from learning how to play football. I painted the ground, cleaned boots, put the kit out. It was all character building, fostered respect and team spirit, but the kids aren't allowed to do any of that nowadays. Every morning, we'd meet at the training ground and collect the kit from the old drying ovens. We'd roll the kit up in a smelly towel and lay it out on the treatment table. The shirts and shorts would be stinking and stiff as boards, and you'd see the players rubbing their socks together to remove the dried mud. They didn't have a choice, because they only had one set of training kit for the season.

Brian Clough used to get apprentices to do his gardening. Obviously, it was free labour, but it was also about getting to know the kids. His wife Barbara would make them tea and sandwiches. Cloughie would also get them to walk his dog. Gary Charles was walking Del Boy once, let him off the lead and lost him. Gary looked for Del Boy all afternoon but couldn't find him, so eventually had to go back to Cloughie's house to break the news to him. As you can imagine, poor old Gary was standing on the doorstep shitting himself. When Cloughie opened the door, Del Boy was asleep in the hallway.

It's a shame that more people in my age range aren't involved in football, not necessarily as managers, but at least working with and advising younger ones. If the chairman's getting on their back, or a player's acting up, it would be good to have someone around to say, 'Listen, calm down, why don't you try doing this, that or the other?' The League Managers Association runs courses where older guys go along and mentor young managers. But there's a lot of pride involved and a lot of young people want to do things their way.

Apparently, Alex Ferguson went back to Old Trafford recently and had a big talk with their current manager Ole Gunnar Solskjær and his staff. I'm told they were chatting for two hours. That kind of advice coming from someone like Fergie is absolutely priceless. Because although you might already think you're good enough, there's always more learning to be done.

24

CRIME AND PUNISHMENT

'We'd settle it with a punch-up ... '

When I left junior school, one of my teachers, Mr Enniver, said to me, 'Be careful, Harry, or you'll end up in the wrong crowd and in prison.' Luckily, Mr Enniver was sport barmy, a big football lover and a nice man who nurtured my talent. So I never flirted with a life of crime, unlike so many other people from the East End. I was a runner, not a fighter. Just because you had a tough upbringing, that doesn't mean you have to end up a villain.

I don't know what's gone wrong with the East End – you hear about stabbings up there every week. Not too long ago, my mate's kid and one of his pals were walking home from the pictures in Stratford and seven kids pulled up on bikes and surrounded them.

They got them up against a wall, pulled out a knife as long as your arm and nicked their coats, trainers, watches, wallets, phones, the lot. I even get a bit scared when I see these gangs of kids now.

I'm told these kids say they carry knives because everyone else carries a knife. It's just not the way to live your life. The only way to stop it is to say, 'If you're caught carrying a knife, you've got to be prepared to be banged up.' Some of the youngsters were talking about it in the jungle, saying how bad it is that black kids are always being stopped. But what are the police supposed to do? If they suspect someone of having a knife, whatever colour they are, you've got to search them. Something has got to be done about it. It's become an epidemic. Every time I pick up a paper there's another story about a kid being stabbed, whether it's in London or another of Britain's towns or cities.

I worry all the time about the world my grandkids are growing up in, because it's got a bit scary out there. You can be in the wrong place at the wrong time and end up dead, just like that. How could you stab someone? I couldn't stick a knife in someone for all the money in the world. It doesn't even bear thinking about. But now kids think nothing of it. Apparently stabbing someone has even got a nickname now: they call it 'splashing'. I assume that means being splashed with blood. There are even people who sing about splashing. Call me old-fashioned if you want, but how sick is that?

When I was growing up in the East End, it was a tough place. And if you went down the wrong path and signed up for a life of crime, then there was a chance you'd come a cropper. It was a case of live by the sword, die by the sword. But innocent kids minding their own business wouldn't end up stabbed to death. When two kids had a falling out in my day, word would go round that there was a fight happening and everyone would come out after school, gather in a big circle, shout and cheer as Charlie Brown and Freddie Smith went at it, hammer and tongs. But nobody would be pulling out a knife. And it wasn't just kids, if two men had a grievance in those days, they'd settle it with a punch-up.

Of course, there were proper villains in my day, people like the Kray twins. But back then, villains were villains. You knew who they were and not to mix with them. And it wasn't as if the Krays went around stabbing strangers in the street. They committed violence, but it was contained. I used to see the Krays in the Grave Maurice on Whitechapel Road, just down from the Blind Beggar. The Blind Beggar was very busy and buzzy, but the Grave Maurice was classy, a little bit quieter and more like a pub up West. They'd play Frank Sinatra, Tony Bennett and all those American crooners. And the Krays would be sat tucked away out the back, minding their own business. They wouldn't be saying to people, 'Who you looking at?' and starting on ordinary people. Don't get me wrong, they weren't nice people, but they only did harm to other villains. They would have been appalled by what's going on up there now.

At the Spirit of London Awards a few years ago, I was intro-duced to a guy called Mark Prince, whose son Kiyan was stabbed to death in London in 2006. Kiyan was only 15, had been trying to break up a fight outside his school and was murdered in front of hundreds of other kids. He wasn't looking to buy drugs or start trouble, he was just minding his own business. Kiyan was a good footballer who played for QPR's youth team and had his whole life ahead of him. When I went and managed QPR, everybody said what a fantastic young talent he was. Apparently, he was powerful and strong as an ox. They also said what a great young man he was. Had he not been killed that day, Kiyan might have been at the peak of a great football career today. You never know, I might even have managed him and we might have ended up as friends.

Mark, a former boxer who fought for the world cruiserweight title, started the Kiyan Prince Foundation, which campaigns against youth violence. He visits schools and prisons talking about knife crime, and I was taken by what an amazing man he is, dedicating his life to trying to make the world a safer place for kids, having lost his boy in such tragic circumstances. Mark is the man, what he's doing is incredible. We need a lot more people like him.

I sat down with Mark and a group of parents who lost their kids to knife crime, and it was very moving listening to all their stories. It was just so, so sad. I spoke to one fella from a quiet little town in Kent who worked with his two boys in a shoe mender's. Every lunchtime, his boys would pop down to the bakery around the corner and get sandwiches. One day, this kid walked into the bakery, started on the two brothers and one of them ended up with a glass tray being smashed into his neck. While he was bleeding to death in the bakery, his dad was wondering where he'd got to. Eventually, his mum went to the bakery to find out where he was, and when she arrived, it was all cordoned off and police were everywhere. She knew straightaway that something terrible had happened. If her son had turned up to the bakery five minutes later, he'd have probably been alright. It's just bad luck, which is what makes it even scarier. Their son's murderer got life, but he'll probably be out in eight years.

I just couldn't imagine what it must be like as a parent – one of my kids going out one night and never coming home again. One minute you've got a son or a daughter, the next you haven't. And these really are just kids. So many of the victims and the boys and girls carrying knives are aged between 10 and 17. But stabbing someone doesn't just destroy the life of the victim, it destroys the lives of entire families and communities, as well that of the perpetrator. Afterwards, I said to Mark, 'Whenever you need me, I'd love to help in any way I can.'

I can help with fundraising, ask people I know to put money into youth and sports clubs, so we can get kids off the streets and doing something constructive. I'd like to go into schools and juvenile prisons, meet these kids, find out why they do what they do and speak to them about the alternatives. I might be a lot older than them and struggle to understand the way they think, but Mark can see that I have a role to play. I worked my way up from a poor upbringing in east London, had a career in football and made a nice life for myself. These kids have seen me on TV and know that I've worked with some of their heroes, whether it's Rio Ferdinand, Frank Lampard or Jermain Defoe. And I can tell them about people like Raheem Sterling, whose father was murdered and who could have quite easily gone down the wrong road but who made a wonderful career for himself in football instead. I can encourage them and create opportunities. And just the fact I want to speak to them speaks volumes.

Anthony Joshua, Britain's greatest fighter, is another great example. He flirted with crime before deciding to concentrate on boxing, and what a great role model he is now. There have been lots of successful boxers and footballers who were once standing at a crossroads. They had fathers who were involved in crime and mates who carried weapons. But they chose the right path instead. We've got to get the message across to kids that there is a better way to live. And we've got to find out what makes kids want to do such terrible things, which involves trying to reach the parents as well. Because a lot of what is going on is down to the parents. These kids are going out with knives, stabbing and robbing people, and a lot of their parents don't seem to have any idea.

If I hadn't made it as a footballer, I probably would have worked on the docks and stayed in the East End for the rest of my life. Or maybe I would have done the Knowledge and driven a cab. What else was I going to do? I had no skills. There would have been nothing wrong with that anyway, it's what so many of my old mates did. But I don't understand it when I hear kids from the East End saying they've got no opportunities nowadays, because they've got far more opportunities than we ever did. I loved growing up in the East End, it made me who I am. But it wasn't always easy.

25

TECHNOLOGY

'A lot of it is cobblers . . . '

I'm more up with technology than you might think. I can do one of those thumbs-up emojis on my phone. Whenever I get a text, that's my go-to emoji. I'm also on a WhatsApp group – The Jungle 11 – with my old campmates, and every day I get messages about what they're all up to. But, to be honest, that's about the extent of it. Technology is clever, but I'm not sure it's all positive.

My manager put me on Instagram but my granddaughter looks after it for me now. She could be putting anything on there. She's not, is she? But I'd never go on Twitter, I'm told it's full of abuse. Why would anyone want to read it? If anyone says to me, 'Harry, look what someone's said about you in the paper,' I'll say, 'What are you telling me for? I didn't know about it, and what I don't see can't hurt me.'

You've got to remember that when I was growing up, we didn't even have tellies in the house, let alone telephones in our pockets. I can still remember our first telly, which was nine inches with a three-inch magnifying glass that you'd hook over the front. It had one station, the BBC. A programme would finish and someone would say, 'We are now taking a short interlude', and suddenly you'd see a farmer and his horse ploughing a field or some bloke making a pot on a wheel. Every night it was the same, and you didn't even see the potter's face, just his hands. I used to sit there watching this bloke make his pot for half an hour, hoping it would collapse and fall off. It never did, but he never finished it either. No wonder people spent so much time in the pub.

When they brought in ITV, my dad said, 'How stupid! How will we know what side to watch?' He couldn't understand the point of having two channels. God knows what he'd make of it now. His head would explode.

Me and Sandra had a black and white TV for quite a few years after we were married, but I certainly remember buying our first colour one. I was sat in a café opposite Upton Park station with my team-mate Roger Cross when this geezer walked in and said, 'How would you like to buy a colour television?' He was flogging these tellies for £110, which was more than a week's wages. But Roger was keen, and said he could borrow some money off his mum. She owned a sweet shop, which meant she was a high-flying businesswoman in our eyes.

When the bloke turned up a few hours later, he said to me, 'Sorry, Harry, but one of the sets got damaged in the van. Nothing major, just a scratch down the side.'

I said to him, 'Roger can have that one.'

I went to switch it on, and this bloke said, 'Whoa, Harry, you can't just switch it on. It's a very sophisticated piece of technology, you need an expert to do all the tuning.'

So I gave him the money and off he trotted.

Luckily, I had a mate who repaired televisions, so I got him round to take a look. When he pressed the on button, nothing happened. He gave it a bang, still nothing. In the end, he unscrewed the panel at the back to reveal absolutely nothing inside. I'd spent £110 on an empty wooden cabinet. When I went round Roger's, his was the same.

When I started playing, the only football on the telly was the FA Cup final and *Match of the Day* on a Saturday night, which back then only showed highlights of one game. The first time we had live League football was when ITV introduced *The Big Match Live* with Brian Moore in the early 1980s. Suddenly, everyone would be glued to their screens of a Sunday afternoon. It's amazing when you think about it now, when you can watch live football from all over the world almost whenever you want, but that's how it was then.

When I want to have a bet, I phone them up. I don't know how to use all these online websites. Until a couple of years ago, I still had one of those old Nokia phones. But towards the end of my career as a manager, there was a lot of stuff being done on computers. I had people doing analysis and stats and stuff like that, and it was handy in terms of seeing how the opposition set up and working out their set plays. But a lot of it is cobblers. There's so much spin and jargon in football nowadays, and bullshit baffles brains.

I was more concerned with how my team played than what a computer told me about the opposition. When I was at Tottenham, all I was worried about was getting the ball to Gareth Bale so that he could rip the opposition to pieces. That's got nothing to do with computers. Nobody ever coached Gareth to pick the ball up, run 70 yards with it, beat four people and smash it into the back of the net, that's just what he could do. Luka Modrić could see a pass like nobody else and never gave the ball away, and I didn't teach him that either.

I preferred to watch a player and let my eyes be the judge. Alex Ferguson would have been the same, he'd have made decisions based on what he saw on the pitch instead of what he saw on a computer screen. You can look at stats until they're coming out of your ears, but if you've been in the game long enough, you get a feel for a player. At one club, I said after training one day, 'Such and such didn't work hard enough.' And the fitness coach replied, 'His heart monitor reading is okay.' But I could see that he hadn't run about enough, I didn't need a heart monitor to tell me.

More and more, football is being run by computer experts, academics and people who have studied coaching and can talk a good game, rather than proper football people who have played the game and understand the reality. Obviously, people like José Mourinho and Arsène Wenger have proved that you can be a very successful manager without having played top-level football. But even Mourinho and Wenger played at a half-decent level before deciding to concentrate on coaching. But there are more and more young coaches coming through who have hardly kicked a ball. I find that strange, especially if you're coaching young kids. If you've never done it, it must be difficult. I see these young coaches on the touchline, in their early 20s, and think, 'Why aren't they out playing football?' I can only assume it's because they can't.

But while you can go overboard with technology and all the different backroom staff, it has its place. Early on in my management career, I'd be out watching a game every night of the week, looking for new players. You were always hopeful of finding a golden nugget, someone like Stuart Pearce at non-league Wealdstone or Ian Wright at non-league Greenwich Borough. But it's a global game now, so managers can't do that.

Now, you'll go in on Monday morning and someone will come and tell you about a promising full-back at some obscure team in Peru. Within seconds, they'll have him up on a screen. Within minutes, you'll know everything about him and have watched him play. The manager might speak to people who have worked with him, and together with the director of football and the chairman or chief executive, they'll make the decision whether to buy him or not. Years ago, a manager would have been ridiculed if they'd admitted to buying a player without seeing him play in the flesh. Now, it's the norm.

But I'm not one of these grumpy old men who goes around saying, 'Things were better in my day.' I was in the barber's recently and this bloke was going on and on about 'kids today' and how rubbish everything is. But the way I see it, things just change. And some things are better, some things are worse. You get in your car now and you've got a nice radio and air conditioning. Years ago, you'd have an old radio with wires hanging out of it that didn't work properly, the battery would keep going flat and you wouldn't be able to start it in the winter. And that was if you were driving John Bond's old Jaguar.

When I was a boy, we'd be out playing football all day, because a football was all we had and there was only one channel on TV. Do kids talk to each other as much as they used to? I'm not sure they do. They're all on these computer games all day. When I go out for dinner with my grandkids, I'll say to them, 'Oi! You ain't spoke to us yet. Do you mind putting your phone down for five minutes and having a chat with your grandparents?' Sometimes they look at me like I'm mad.

But it's not just little kids who play computer games, footballers play them as well. Either that or they're looking at their phones. We used to be on the coach playing cards, talking about football and having a laugh. You can't go around saying to footballers, 'Stop playing computer games, stop listening to your music, don't do this, that and the other.' That's just the way it is now, and you end up sounding like their granddad. But I do think the way they are now is corrosive to team spirit. Players nowadays are a lot quieter than they used to be, and quite a few of them have no interest in football beyond their own experience of it. Just have a chat, you're supposed to be team-mates.

26
FOREIGNERS

'If you don't adapt, you get found out ...'

Just because I was born and raised in the East End and don't claim to be a wine connoisseur doesn't mean I'm a caveman. I might have started out in management with Bournemouth in 1983, when they were in the old Third Division and a player from Wales was considered to be a little bit glamorous, but when I was managing in the Premier League, I was dealing with players from all over the world. Huge changes happened very quickly in English football in the 1990s, and if you didn't adapt as a manager, you got found out.

Suddenly, I was dealing with foreign players from very different footballing cultures. While British players were still very much into their drinking well into the 1990s, and most clubs still had their Tuesday drinking clubs, most of the foreign players that came in were total professionals and looked after themselves like the athletes they were supposed to be. Even when I arrived at Tottenham in 2008, I had players getting into trouble in nightclubs. I didn't want to be waking up on a Sunday morning, someone phoning me up and telling me that one of my players was in the papers for being drunk and disorderly. And it was almost always British players. The foreigners didn't drink, went to bed early, ate healthily and were fit as fiddles. That meant the British players had to change their ways to keep up, and that also meant the British managers had to find different ways of managing.

The days of throwing tea cups around the dressing room were gone, and there was no point in effing and blinding at a lad from Colombia who could hardly speak English. Foreign players just weren't used to being shouted at or embarrassed in front of their team-mates. And there was no point in using old-fashioned bullying tactics, because it would only turn them against you. If I'd kicked a tray of sandwiches and the sandwiches had landed on a foreign player's head – as happened when I was having a row with Don Hutchison in the dressing room at West Ham – that probably would have been the end of that relationship. Don barely even noticed it had happened.

When I signed Paolo Di Canio for West Ham, someone wrote in the paper that I was walking a tightrope with no safety net. In fact, even when I told the chairman Terry Brown that I wanted to sign him, he put his head in his hands and said, 'Anybody but him.' When he was playing for Sheffield Wednesday, Paolo pushed over a referee. He had a reputation as a loose cannon. Nobody else wanted him because they thought he was crazy. But I never had any doubts about signing him. I loved watching him play at Sheffield Wednesday, not so much when he was playing against my team.

Paolo wasn't a wrong 'un but working with him was a challenge. Every day you had to be on your toes, because you wouldn't know what kind of mood he'd be in. One day he'd walk into the dressing room wearing sunglasses and singing 'Volare', the next he'd kick the door and start ranting and raving about how rubbish everything was. You were always on eggshells with Paolo.

Paolo was one of the best trainers I ever saw. He'd come in on Sunday mornings with his own fitness coach, who he brought over from Italy, and be there for two hours, working on his movement or the quickness of his feet. He was in unbelievable shape. You could almost put your fingers around his waist. Because of Paolo, other players started to stretch properly and conditioning became a thing. By the end of Paolo's first season, a lot of the lads were eating their own tailored meals. But getting Paolo to gel with some of the other stuff that was still going on in English football was a real challenge for me. I wouldn't say he was uncontrollable, but he was very high maintenance.

When I picked the teams in training, I'd always make sure Stuart Pearce, Razor Ruddock and all the other nutters were on his side, so that they wouldn't boot him and it would all kick off. When he shot wide, I'd say it was a goal. He'd storm off the training field complaining that Razor was mucking about too much: 'Hey, gaffer! We are warming up, we are supposed to be stretching, and

Razor is laughing all the time. He is saying he drank 12 pints of beer last night and talking about who he was shagging. How can this be right?'

And I'd have to tell him that I'd sort it out, because I needed him on my side. And the other lads learnt so much by playing with and watching him work.

It was about creating the right atmosphere to make Paolo feel important. He was our best player, and you've got to make allowances for people like him. On any given Saturday, he was likely to be our match-winner, so I had to keep him sweet during the week. He could suddenly turn the game, bring the ball out of the sky, shape to hit the ball with his left foot, put a defender on his backside, bring the ball back the other way and slot it in the corner. He was just beautifully balanced and his technique was immaculate. Even when I took a side to Old Trafford when Man Utd at their peak – with Ryan Giggs, Paul Scholes, David Beckham, Eric Cantona and the rest in their team – I always thought we had a chance with Paolo in our side.

Paolo didn't like playing away from home much, especially if it meant having to get a flight. Once, we were playing at Sheffield Wednesday and when we got to Stansted, there was a problem with our plane. Everyone else was sitting patiently on the plane, waiting for the problem to be fixed, but Paolo kept going on at me: 'Gaffer, I don't like this plane. This plane is shit. Why are we on this plane?'

After a while, this old van pulled up next to the plane and two skinheads jumped out, wearing earrings and with tattoos all up their legs. Paolo came running down the aisle and started screaming, 'Hey, boss, I don't want to die!'

'Don't worry, Paolo, they're gonna fix the plane.'

'Boss, they couldn't fix my bike!'

With that, Paolo was off out the exit and running down the runway. The club secretary had to chase after him and go with him in a car to Sheffield.

When we played Bradford in 2000, we were 4–2 down with 25 minutes left. Paolo had a few penalty appeals turned down, started running towards me and demanding to be substituted. Next thing I know, he's sat in front of the dugout, sulking: 'I don't play. I come off.'

I was shouting at him, 'Paolo, get up, get up. We're losing 4–2 to Bradford. Please, Paolo, get back on the pitch and get on with the game.' That might not be exactly what I said, but you get the picture. Eventually Paolo did get up, scored a penalty and set up the winner.

And in a story you couldn't make up, I was ordered to substitute Paolo after he sparked a 17-man brawl during Julian Dicks's testimonial. I can only imagine it was some kind of elaborate tribute to Julian. Thankfully, Julian wasn't on the pitch at the time, because he probably would have got sent off.

For all the aggravation, I loved working with Paolo. He was just so passionate about football. Even in training, he was like a little kid in the playground. Every time there was a corner or a free-kick, he'd been running over and wrestling the ball out of someone's hands. He loved West Ham and the fans loved him back. He also could have been a legend at any other club in the Premier League, but nobody else wanted to take that chance.

What also changed were the age-old methods of building team spirit. In the old days, it was all very simple: you'd all go out for a drink, swap stories, fall about laughing, get into some scrapes and all go home again. Even when I was managing in the Premier League, I'd sometimes round the lads up for a day at the races, followed by a meal and a glass of wine in a nice Italian restaurant. That's what I did at Portsmouth in 2006, the season we managed to stay up after looking doomed, and I did the same after I took over at Tottenham in 2008. Spurs had only won two points from their first eight matches, but after a day out at Cheltenham, we won three and drew one of our next four.

Before Portsmouth played Cardiff in the 2008 FA Cup final, I took the lads down to an Italian restaurant in Windsor. Ring any bells? That's right, it wasn't much different to how me and the Bournemouth lads prepared before our upset of Manchester United in the third round of the 1984 FA Cup. The Portsmouth lads even got stuck into some karaoke. John Utaka, who set up Kanu for his winning goal the following afternoon at Wembley, did Bob Marley's 'No Woman, No Cry', and Hermann Hreiðarsson had packed his white Elvis jumpsuit and had us rolling in the aisles with his impersonation.

Utaka was Nigerian and Hreiðarsson was from Iceland, which proves that foreign players were still up for doing things the old way. Not that I ever did a Brian Clough. Before his Notts Forest side played Southampton in the 1979 League Cup final, Cloughie locked his players in a room with half-a-dozen bottles of champagne and wouldn't let any of them leave until it was all gone. When they played holders Liverpool in the first round of the European Cup earlier that season, they travelled up to Anfield on the day of the match and Cloughie told the driver to pull over so that he could dig out a crate of beer for the players.

But by the time I arrived at Tottenham in 2008, it had become more difficult to bond the players. One day, I took them all to Cheltenham Racecourse. I thought it would be a good way of getting them to relax and have a bit of fun together. But most of the foreign lads weren't interested. You'd have thought I'd taken them on a prison visit. Roman Pavlyuchenko, our Russian striker, just sat there all day, waiting for someone to tell him to get back on the coach. Roman was an amazing talent, could score amazing goals, but he always was a bit laid-back. The first day I arrived at Tottenham's training ground, we had a little practice game and I kept shouting at him to make runs. I didn't know who anyone was, but this guy in a tracksuit kept running onto the pitch and talking to Roman. So I said to one of the other players, 'Who's this geezer?'

'Oh, that's his interpreter ... '

The interpreter ended up running about more than Roman.

For decades, foreign players just weren't part of the English football culture. So when they first started flooding into English football in the 1990s, most British managers, including me, didn't have a clue how to look after them. You'd buy a midfielder from Nigeria or Ecuador, dump them in a house somewhere and expect them to do the business on the pitch on Saturday. We didn't understand that these people needed looking after. Just because someone might have been a superstar player in his own country didn't mean he was going to come in and start being a superstar in England.

We might hire someone to teach them the language, but these players also had wives who couldn't speak English. They didn't have any friends and were sitting in a house all day on their own, not even able to watch TV. What about the kids and their schooling? What about the shopping? Where to go for a nice meal or coffee? Or someone to introduce the wife to new friends? But because we'd paid millions of pounds for a player, we thought that if he wasn't performing, that was his problem.

Javier Margas was a defender from Chile who I signed for West Ham in 1998. Margas had played all four of his country's games at the 1998 World Cup and I thought he'd be able to do a job for us in the Premier League. He came over with his wife, we bought them a car and a house, dumped them in it and that was it. The house was out near Brentwood in Essex, about ten miles from the training ground in Chadwell Heath, and we just expected him to turn up the following morning, even though he'd never driven on that side of the road and had no satnav or even a map. Unsurprisingly, Javier got lost and ended up at Stansted Airport, which is about 40 miles in the wrong direction. He eventually turned up, but got lost again on his way home and ended up with a puncture down some country lane. And that was just the start of it.

Javier's wife came from a very wealthy family in Chile. Her father owned a chain of hotels, including the biggest in Santiago, and was very close to her parents and sisters. One minute she's living this lovely life, seeing her family and friends every day, and now she's stuck in a house in Essex, without a word of English and nobody to talk to even if she could speak the language. So Javier started coming into my office and telling me that his wife was depressed and crying all day. Before long, his wife had gone back to Chile, and Javier was on his own. And not long after that, he moved into a hotel in Waltham Abbey.

One day, he didn't turn up for training, so we arranged a meeting at this hotel. When me and West Ham's managing director Peter Storrie arrived, we asked the receptionist to ring his room, but we got no answer. We rang and rang and rang, before asking to be shown to his room and knocking on his door. Still no answer. We went back to reception, told them he wasn't answering, and another receptionist insisted that Javier had come in about half an hour earlier and asked for his door key. Anyway, we persuaded this guy to open up his room for us, and when we walked in, the window was wide open and it was obvious that Javier had jumped out and legged it. He'd left all his clothes behind, his kit and his boots, and presumably just taken his passport and whatever he was wearing. I never saw him again. Peter went out to Chile and tried to persuade him to come back, but he wasn't having it. We tried to sell him back to his old club, but Javier decided to retire instead.

Some of the time in those early days, the problem was me not understanding a player's needs. There was no proper care, and I have to take the blame for some of the situations that panned out. But the most important aspect of any kind of management, whether it's managing a football team or a team in an office environment, is to learn from your mistakes.

It was a sad situation with Javier because he was a nice lad, a good player and, with the right care, he could have been a great asset for West Ham. Instead, it turned into a disaster for him and for us. It was only later on – when we all realised that dumping someone from Chile in a house, giving him a car, expecting him to turn up to training the next day and play like a dream on Saturday was ridiculous – that player liaison officers came into the game. Now, all the clubs have player liaison officers. When I was at Tottenham, there were a couple of them. They'd speak lots of languages, and if a player's boiler was up the spout, the flush had gone on his toilet or his baby was unwell and needed a doctor, they'd get someone in to fix it. That made perfect sense to me.

But there were a few foreign imports who only had themselves to blame for their failings. There was Marco Boogers, who I signed for West Ham in 1995 and was an absolute nightmare. In fact, he might be my worst ever signing. All he used to say was, 'We don't do this in Holland, we don't do that in Holland.' When I threw him on against Man Utd, he almost chopped Gary Neville in half with his first tackle and got sent off. He only played a couple more games before going back to Holland.

When I signed Paulo Futre for West Ham in 1996, he had a reputation as one of the best players in the world. He was a Portuguese international, had won the European Cup with Porto, played for some of the biggest clubs in Europe and was one of the most technically gifted players I'd ever seen. In training he was incredible. He was getting stuck in, taking the free-kicks, taking the corners, so I picked him to start in the first game of the season against Arsenal.

When we arrived at Highbury, I took the team-sheets to their manager Arsène Wenger, but a few minutes later, our kitman told me we had a problem with Futre: 'He won't wear the number 16. He threw it back in my face.' We were 45 minutes away from kick-off, so I found Futre and said to him, 'Paulo, we've got squad numbers now. You're number 16 for the season, we can't change it.' But Paulo wasn't having any of it.

He said to me, 'Futre – 10. Pelé, Eusébio, Maradona – 10. No fucking 16.'

'But, Paulo, your number was already gone when you arrived at West Ham. John Moncur has the number 10 shirt.'

'No fucking 16.'

'Look, Paulo, it's ten past two and we've got a big game. The sun's shining, it's a full house, please just get your gear on and we'll talk about it Monday.'

'No talk. No fucking 16.'

This conversation was taking place in the middle of the dressing room, so all the other players were looking at us and it was getting embarrassing. Anyway, Paulo threw his shirt on the floor, trod on it and kicked it up in the air. And with that, he was gone.

Frank Lampard Sr said to me, 'Well done, Harry.'

'Well done? What's it got to do with me?'

'Well, what we gonna do?'

'We'll just have to tell the referee we're changing the team.'

'Are we allowed to do that?'

'Yeah, course we are … '

So I went into the referee's office and said, 'You won't believe this, ref, but Frank Lampard's filled the team-sheet in wrong. He's put Paulo Futre down and he's not even here.' I was right about that, because he was probably halfway to the airport by then.

Arsène was a bit suspicious at first – 'What are these tactics?' – but he let us off and they ended up beating us 2–0.

On the Monday, Futre came into training with his agent and his solicitors. He wouldn't budge, and even offered to pay £100,000 for the number 10 shirt.

I said to him, 'Paulo, lots of kids have already paid for West Ham shirts with number 10 and "Moncur" written on the back. What about them?'

'I pay for them. How many have you sold?'

'I think about 50,000.'

We'd probably sold about ten. In the end, he gave John Moncur a two-week holiday in his villa in the Algarve in exchange for the number 10 shirt. About a month later, Paulo did his knee and that was the end of him.

Florin Răducioiu had a great World Cup for Romania in 1994 and I decided to buy him for West Ham after a decent European Championship two years later. But I thought I might have problems with him when he kept asking about the quarantine arrangements for his dog during the transfer negotiations.

He actually impressed me in the early training sessions, but the moment it got a bit physical, he didn't fancy it one bit. Julian Dicks was keen to get stuck into him, but Răducioiu wouldn't go anywhere near him. After a couple of friendlies, Răducioiu walked off the pitch almost crying about the rough treatment he was getting, and I'd pretty much given up on him before the season had started. One training session, even Paulo Futre called Florin a big girl.

The final straw was when Răducioiu didn't turn up for a League Cup match away at Stockport County. It was snowing heavily, Iain Dowie scored an incredible header, except in the wrong goal, and we lost the game. The next day, someone phoned me up and told me they'd seen Florin out shopping with his wife in Harvey Nichols in London. I wish I'd gone shopping with him.

Florin has since admitted he should have tried harder to adapt to the English game, but I hold my hands up as well, because I should have shown more patience and understanding of the difficulties he was experiencing. It's not just football that has become more multicultural, it's society in general. And for us all to get along, we've got to take the time to understand each other.

27
REGRETS

'The longer you're here, the more
you learn ...'

There's a Muhammad Ali quote I like: 'A man who views the world at 50 the same as he did at 20 has wasted 30 years of his life.' I look back at things I did and the way I acted when I was younger and think, that would never happen now. The longer you're here, the more you learn about life and people.

I do sometimes look back and think I could have done things differently, but I don't have many regrets. One regret I do have is how things panned out with me as manager of West Ham. West Ham had been my team since I was a kid and I had a great group of players coming through. Six of them – Rio Ferdinand, Frank

Lampard, Michael Carrick, Jermain Defoe, Joe Cole and Glen Johnson – went on to play for England, and if I could have kept them together, that West Ham team could have gone on to do anything. But when Rio was sold to Leeds against my wishes, everything started to unravel. I knew that Rio would become the best centre-half in Europe and I begged him not to go, but he was being pushed out of the door. The chairman Terry Brown thought he'd never see that kind of money again – Rio went for £18 million, which was a British transfer record – and soon Frank Lampard left as well.

I still didn't intend on going anywhere, but not long after signing a new four-year contract, I did an interview with a fanzine. These four lads came into my office, I was chatting away to them, and one of them said, 'Terry Brown reckons you've already spent £14 million of Rio Ferdinand's transfer fee.' And I replied, ''E's supposed to be a fuckin' accountant and he can't even add up. What chance have we got?' It wasn't a nice thing to say. Unfortunately for me, Terry read absolutely everything, including the fanzines. The following week, after we'd just beaten Southampton, I went in to see him about my new contract and he said, 'I'm not happy, Harry, I think we should call it a day.' And that was that, my time at West Ham was over – as was Frank Lampard Sr's, which I felt bad about.

I was young, cocky and headstrong, and probably a bit disrespectful to Terry. I'd walk into a board meeting, someone would say something and I'd reply, 'What do you know about football?' I found it very difficult to bite my tongue, but as Sandra used to remind me quite a lot, they owned the football club and I was their employee. I completely lost it with Terry once, when he suggested I was only playing my nephew Frank Lampard so that he could collect appearance money. Terry was obviously talking rubbish – look how good Frank became – but I should never have spoken to him like I did.

When I was at Southampton, the chairman Rupert Lowe, who was a proper toff, used to try to tell me how to play the game. I'd say to him, 'What do you know about football? You played hockey.' I should have just sucked it up. You've got to be diplomatic as a manager. Look at Mauricio Pochettino at Tottenham: he doesn't complain publicly about not having money to spend, he just gets on with it. That was something I learned with age and experience.

Players can be very precious nowadays. If you criticise them, their agent will be on the phone to you the following day. When I was manager at Tottenham, Darren Bent missed an absolute sitter. So when I was interviewed after the game, I said, 'My missus could have scored that.' It was only tongue in cheek, but his agent got the hump and raised it with the chairman. For 80 grand a week, I didn't think it was asking too much of Darren to score an open goal from two yards out. And I was only saying what millions of other blokes watching the game were saying. But I did regret it, because I liked Darren and he was a good player, and it ruined our relationship. You just can't get away with saying stuff like that nowadays. It doesn't matter if the player is British or foreign, a player might take it the wrong way and stop playing for you.

Not long after Darren left Tottenham, I did some work with a young manager at Derby. And who's at the club? Darren Bent, and he'd probably told everyone how much he hated me. As I was walking out onto the training ground, Benty hit one from about 30 yards out and it went right in the top corner. It was the best volley I'd ever seen. So I shouted, 'Benty, my old woman couldn't have scored that!' Thankfully, he started laughing.

Even in the jungle I had to watch what I said at times. Sair did a trial and only won a few stars, so when she got back to the camp I said to her, 'Rita will beat you up when she finds out!' But everyone else was telling me to shut up, because Sair was upset. I couldn't see why it was anything to worry about. I can take the piss out of myself and I don't mind it when people take the piss out of me. When I went in the jungle, I got texts from people asking if I was going to take Niko Kranjčar or Peter Crouch in there with me, because they'd both played for me at lots of different clubs. I find that sort of stuff funny. But, as I have only recently started to work out, not everyone does.

Another thing I wish I'd known when I was younger is the benefit of patience. You've got to be patient with players and, most importantly, spend time talking to them. My one piece of advice to young managers would be, 'Get to know your youngsters.' Find out what's going on in their lives, how their digs are, how things are at home. When Stevie Gerrard first started coaching the kids over at Liverpool, I said to him, 'Every day, have a chat with one or two of them. Ask them how their life is and whether they've got any problems. Spend 20 minutes after training doing individual work with them.' Because you know that they'll go home and say to their parents, 'Mum, Dad, Stevie said I'm doing well, we worked on my finishing together after training, just me and him.' Just that bit of extra attention will make them feel ten feet tall.

But there's no point having too many regrets in life, because you're not the same person who made those past decisions. That's why, with apologies to Frank Sinatra, I've got too few regrets to mention. I did what I had to do.

28
KEEPING ON MOVING

'I'll keep working for as long
as possible ...'

I think that's probably me done in terms of football management. I had a great run, over 30 years. Wherever football took me, I enjoyed it and met so many good people. What a way to make a living, doing something you love and getting paid very well for it. Apart from when I was at Bournemouth. But by the end it was making me a bit weary. I still get the odd offer. I had a phone call the other day from Portugal, but I don't want to go abroad now. We like it where we live and I'm not chasing it anymore. I hope the day never comes when I sit in front of a fire all day with a rug over my knees, staring out of the window at the sea. But you know what? That doesn't have to happen.

There's nothing I'm really striving to do, but every day is full-on, just like it always has been. When it was football, it was non-stop. Now I'm supposed to be retired, I seem to be doing something or other every day. I like going to bed looking forward to doing something, and I love opening my eyes in the morning and thinking, 'Oh yeah, I'm doing that today.' I even did a McDonald's advert with Jamie, which is not something I thought I'd ever do. I've also signed up to do some adverts for a betting company, which is definitely something I thought I might do.

The good thing about getting old is, it makes you want to do more with your days. Once you realise you're not going to be around forever, you don't want to be sitting around doing nothing all day. I'll keep working for as long as possible. Getting out and about, meeting people, giving people my time.

I don't mind watching Jeremy Kyle occasionally, although where he finds those people I do not know. But as for all these reality TV shows – even though I'm told that's what *I'm a Celebrity* was – I'm not interested. *Gogglebox*? People sitting watching other people on TV watching TV? Absolutely crackers.

I'm not a big watcher of films, but if I had to choose a favourite, it would be *The Godfather*. I could watch that over and over again. In terms of music, I love listening to anyone who can actually sing: Frank Sinatra, Tony Bennett, Gladys Knight, Whitney Houston, Céline Dion, Mariah Carey. They remind me of those Friday and Saturday nights in the East End, when every pub would have people up singing. Not that I can sing a note, as you would already know if you heard me doing karaoke and murdering Sinatra in the jungle.

Sandra's not a big one for going away on holiday, she's quite happy at home, but I like to get away when I can. I'll watch almost any sport. I went to the rugby at Twickenham recently, to see England beat France in the Six Nations. I'll watch the cricket and the golf, and I'm a big boxing fan. They've got some bottle, those boys, and I love their approach to training and fitness. Sometimes I'll go to the fights, but I prefer watching it at home with a nice cup of tea. In fact, I prefer to watch most things nowadays with a nice cup of tea.

After the jungle, I signed up to do a tour. It's 30-odd nights, so will be a challenge. But getting up on stage and talking to a crowd of people doesn't bother me at all. I've done it plenty of times before, I could do it standing on my head. And there is someone asking me questions and teeing up my stories, which makes it easier. I've got plenty of stories. Once I start talking, they all start coming out and you can't shut me up. The audience might start shouting, 'Get me out of here!' I'm in Manchester, Liverpool, Leeds, Birmingham, Cardiff, Milton Keynes, Hull and just about everywhere else. I said to the fella who's organising it, 'I don't know if I've taken too much on.' And he said to me, 'Harry, you've got to keep doing things while you can, before you can't anymore.' Perhaps he's right. There will come a time when I'm sitting at home all day doing not a great deal, so I should keep getting out and meeting people.

I also enjoy a round of golf. I started playing too late to get any good at it and I don't play enough, but I'm a 14 handicap. For anyone reading this that doesn't understand golf, that's nothing to write home about. I'm not really made for golf, because I've got no patience. My mate Mervyn takes about ten minutes to hit a putt, but I'm one of those people who walks up to my ball and hits it, without taking any practice swings. That's how to play golf properly.

I enjoy doing bits and pieces of punditry and going to watch Bournemouth with the grandkids. And not just Bournemouth, I'll watch any football. I sit downstairs on a Sunday and watch it all day: English football, Spanish football, Italian football, African football. If I'm walking the dogs over the park and there's a game on, I'll stop and watch it. And I still get the hump if I see a player doing something wrong. I also feel for a manager if I see players being lazy, because I know what it's like to feel let down. I'll be on the edge of the sofa, shouting at the telly: 'Fuckin' 'ell! You learn that as a six-year-old! If someone plays a one-two, you go with the runner!' Sandra will be pottering around in the kitchen next door, and there will be no one else in the room with me. But it's impossible to let go of that passion. I sometimes meet people in football who'll say, 'I didn't watch last night's game, because the missus wanted to watch *EastEnders*.' I just can't understand it.

That emotion I had for the game never faded, and never will. Even at the end, I'd wake up on a Monday morning and just get so excited about what the week might bring. I was like a little kid. If I was taking a team to Anfield on the Wednesday, it would feel like a treat and an adventure to look forward to. I'd still get as high as I ever did after a win and just as low after a loss. A few years ago, I managed a pro-celebrity England team in the Soccer Aid charity game. Kenny Dalglish was managing a Rest of the World team, and we ended up having a proper row on the touchline, because I wanted to bring the singer Craig David back on. How ridiculous must that have looked.

Recently, I did a programme called *Harry's Heroes*. It was set up almost like a heist film, but instead of gangsters, it was about a group of old players – including David Seaman, Chris Waddle, Matt Le Tissier and Robbie Fowler – wanting to get together and play one last game against some veteran Germans. The story followed the early phone calls, the first ramshackle meeting and even a bonding session in Marbella. You can imagine how that went. The first training session was at eight in the morning and a couple of the lads didn't roll in until 5.30. But the passion was still there and we managed to whip them into some kind of shape (apart from Razor Ruddock). I loved doing it and winning that game against the Germans gave me a real buzz.

I've got seven grandkids, ranging from 19 to 10. Jamie's two boys live a couple of hours' drive away, so it's not easy for me to see them, because I lead a busy life. But Mark's kids live up the road from me. We spoil them, especially Sandra. But I just love spending time with them, and watching them play football at the weekend. One of Jamie's boys is at Chelsea's academy and one of Mark's boys is at Bournemouth. They're both doing okay, but it's difficult to say whether any of them will be players, because there are lots of good kids about and it's tough. But they're keen, they enjoy it, and they're the main things.

If my family's okay, I'm okay. You know? And my only ambition for my grandkids is that they grow up to be nice people. That's how I'd like to be remembered, as a nice person who had time for everybody and treated them with respect, whether they were a billionaire or someone sleeping rough on the street. And for being a little bit more than the King of the Jungle!

PICTURE CREDITS